Leonora by Maria Edgeworth

Maria Edgeworth was born at Black Bourton, Oxfordshire on January 1st 1768. Her early years were with her mother's family in England. Sadly, her mother died when Maria was five.

Maria was educated at Mrs Lattafière's school in Derby in 1775. There she studied dancing, French and other subjects. Maria transferred to Mrs Devis's school in Upper Wimpole Street, London. Her father began to focus more attention on Maria in 1781 when she nearly lost her sight to an eye infection.

She returned home to Ireland at 14 and took charge of her younger siblings. She herself was home-tutored by her father in Irish economics and politics, science, literature and law. Despite her youth literature was in her blood. Maria also became her father's assistant in managing the family's large Edgeworthstown estate.

Maria first published 1795 with 'Letters for Literary Ladies'. That same year 'An Essay on the Noble Science of Self-Justification', written for a female audience, advised women on how to obtain better rights in general and specifically from their husbands.

'Practical Education' (1798) is a progressive work on education. Maria's ambition was to create an independent thinker who understands the consequences of his or her actions.

Her first novel, 'Castle Rackrent' was published anonymously in 1800 without her father's knowledge. It was an immediate success and firmly established Maria's appeal to the public.

Her father married four times and the last of these to Frances, a year younger and a confidante of Maria, who pushed them to travel more widely: London, Britain and Europe were all now visited.

The second series of 'Tales of Fashionable Life' (1812) did so well that she was now the most commercially successful novelist of her age.

She particularly worked hard to improve the living standards of the poor in Edgeworthstown and to provide schools for the local children of all and any denomination.

After a visit to see her relations Maria had severe chest pains and died suddenly of a heart attack in Edgeworthstown on 22nd May 1849. She was 81.

Index of Contents

LEONORA

Lady Olivia to Lady Leonora L—.

What a misfortune it is to be born a woman! In vain, dear Leonora, would you reconcile me to my doom. Condemned to incessant hypocrisy, or everlasting misery, woman is the slave or the outcast of society. Confidence in our fellow-creatures, or in ourselves, alike forbidden us, to what purpose have we understandings, which we may not use? hearts, which we may not trust? To our unhappy sex, genius and sensibility are the most treacherous gifts of heaven. Why should we cultivate talents merely to gratify the caprice of tyrants? Why seek for knowledge, which can prove only that our wretchedness is irremediable? If a ray of light break in upon us, it is but to make darkness more visible; to show us the narrow limits, the Gothic structure, the impenetrable barriers of our prison. Forgive me if on this subject I cannot speak—if I cannot think—with patience. Is it not fabled, that the gods, to punish some refractory mortal of the male kind, doomed his soul to inhabit upon earth a female form? A punishment more degrading, or more difficult to endure, could scarcely be devised by cruelty omnipotent. What dangers, what sorrows, what persecutions, what nameless evils await the woman who dares to rise above the prejudices of her sex!

"Ah! happy they, the happiest of their kind!"

who, without a struggle, submit their reason to be swathed by all the absurd bandages of custom. What, though they cripple or distort their minds; are not these deformities beauties in the eyes of fashion? and are not these people the favoured nurselings of the World, secure of her smiles, her caresses, her fostering praise, her partial protection, through all the dangers of youth and all the dotage of age?

"Ah! happy they, the happiest of their kind!"

who learn to speak, and think, and act by rote; who have a phrase, or a maxim, or a formula ready for every occasion; who follow—

"All the nurse and all the priest have taught."

And is it possible that Olivia can envy these tideless-blooded souls their happiness—their apathy? Is her high spirit so broken by adversity? Not such the promise of her early years, not such the language of her unsophisticated heart! Alas! I scarcely know, I scarcely recollect, that proud self, which was wont to defy the voice of opinion, and to set at nought the decrees of prejudice. The events of my life shall be related, or rather the history of my sensations; for in a life like mine, sensations become events—a metamorphosis which you will see in every page of my history. I feel an irresistible impulse to open my whole heart to you, my dear Leonora. I ought to be awed by the superiority of your understanding and of your character; yet there is an indulgence in your nature, a softness in your temper, that dissipates fear, and irresistibly attracts confidence.

You have generously refused to be prejudiced against me by busy, malignant rumour; you have resolved to judge of me for yourself. Nothing, then, shall be concealed. In such circumstances I cannot seek to extenuate any of my faults or follies. I am ready to acknowledge them all with self-humiliation more poignant than the sarcasms of my bitterest enemies. But I must pause till I have summoned courage for my confession. Dear Leonora, adieu!

OLIVIA.

OLIVIA TO LEONORA.

Full of life and spirits, with a heart formed for all the enthusiasm, for all the delicacy of love, I married early, in the fond expectation of meeting a heart suited to my own. Cruelly disappointed, I found— merely a husband. My heart recoiled upon itself; true to my own principles of virtue, I scorned dissimulation. I candidly confessed to my husband, that my love was extinguished. I proved to him, alas! too clearly, that we were not born for each other. The attractive moment of illusion was past—never more to return; the repulsive reality remained. The living was chained to the dead, and, by the inexorable tyranny of English laws, that chain, eternally galling to innocence, can be severed only by the desperation of vice. Divorce, according to our barbarous institutions, cannot be obtained without guilt. Appalled at the thought, I saw no hope but in submission. Yet to submit to live with the man I could not love was, to a mind like mine, impossible. My principles and my feelings equally revolted from this legal prostitution. We separated. I sought for balm to my wounded heart in foreign climes.

To the beauties of nature I was ever feelingly alive. Amidst the sublime scenes of Switzerland, and on the consecrated borders of her classic lakes, I sometimes forgot myself to happiness. Felicity, how transient!—transient as the day-dreams that played upon my fancy in the bright morning of love. Alas! not all creation's charms could soothe me to repose. I wandered in search of that which change of place cannot afford. There was an aching void in my heart—an indescribable sadness over my spirits. Sometimes I had recourse to books; but how few were in unison with my feelings, or touched the trembling chords of my disordered mind! Commonplace morality I could not endure. History presented nothing but a mass of crimes. Metaphysics promised some relief, and I bewildered myself in their not inelegant labyrinth. But to the bold genius and exquisite pathos of some German novelists I hold myself indebted for my largest portion of ideal bliss; for those rapt moments, when sympathy with kindred souls transported me into better worlds, and consigned vulgar realities to oblivion.

I am well aware, my Leonora, that you approve not of these my favourite writers: but yours is the morality of one who has never known sorrow. I also would interdict such cordials to the happy. But would you forbid those to taste felicity in dreams who feel only misery when awake? Would you dash the cup of Lethe from lips to which no other beverage is salubrious or sweet?

By the use of these opiates my soul gradually settled into a sort of pleasing pensive melancholy. Has it not been said, that melancholy is a characteristic of genius? I make no pretensions to genius: but I am persuaded that melancholy is the habitual, perhaps the natural state of those who have the misfortune to feel with delicacy.

You, my dear Leonora, will class this notion amongst what you once called my refined errors. Indeed I must confess, that I see in you an exception so striking as almost to compel me to relinquish my theory. But again let me remind you, that your lot in life has been different from mine. Alas! how different! Why had not I such a friend, such a mother as yours, early to direct my uncertain steps, and to educate me to happiness? I might have been—But no matter what I might have been—. I must tell you what I have been.

Separated from my husband, without a guide, without a friend at the most perilous period of my life, I was left to that most insidious of counsellors—my own heart—my own weak heart. When I was least prepared to resist the impression, it was my misfortune to meet with a man of a soul congenial with my own. Before I felt my danger, I was entangled beyond the possibility of escape. The net was thrown over my heart; its struggles were to no purpose but to exhaust my strength. Virtue commanded me to be miserable—and I was miserable. But do I dare to expect your pity, Leonora, for such an attachment? It excites your indignation, perhaps your horror. Blame, despise, detest me; all this would I rather bear, than deceive you into fancying me better than I really am.

Do not, however, think me worse. If my views had been less pure, if I had felt less reliance on the firmness of my own principles, and less repugnance to artifice, I might easily have avoided some appearances, which have injured me in the eyes of the world. With real contrition I confess, that a fatal mixture of masculine independence of spirit, and of female tenderness of heart, has betrayed me into many imprudences; but of vice, and of that meanest species of vice, hypocrisy, I thank Heaven, my conscience can acquit me. All I have now to hope is, that you, my indulgent, my generous Leonora, will not utterly condemn me. Truth and gratitude are my only claims to your friendship—to a friendship, which would be to me the first of earthly blessings, which might make me amends for all I have lost. Consider this before, unworthy as I am, you reject me from your esteem. Counsel, guide, save me! Without vanity, but with confidence I say it, I have a heart that will repay you for affection. You will find me easily moved, easily governed by kindness. Yours has already sunk deep into my soul, and your power is unlimited over the affections and over the understanding of

Your obliged

OLIVIA.

LETTER III

FROM LADY LEONORA L— TO HER MOTHER, THE DUCHESS OF —, ENCLOSING THE PRECEDING LETTERS.

I am permitted to send you, my dear mother, the enclosed letters. Mixed with what you may not approve, you will, I think, find in them proofs of an affectionate heart and superior abilities. Lady Olivia is just returned to England. Scandal, imported from the continent, has had such an effect in prejudicing many of her former friends and acquaintance against her, that she is in danger of being excluded from that society of which she was once the ornament and the favourite; but I am determined to support her cause, and to do every thing in my power to counteract the effects of malignity. I cannot sufficiently express the indignation that I feel against the mischievous spirit of scandal, which destroys happiness at every breath, and which delights in the meanest of all malignant feelings—the triumph over the errors of superior characters. Olivia has been much blamed, because she has been much envied.

Indeed, my dear mother, you have been prejudiced against her by false reports. Do not imagine that her fascinating manners have blinded my judgment: I assure you that I have discerned, or rather that she has revealed to me, all her faults: and ought not this candour to make a strong impression upon my mind in her favour? Consider how young, how beautiful she was at her first entrance into fashionable life; how much exposed to temptation, surrounded by flatterers, and without a single friend. I am persuaded that she would have escaped all censure, and would have avoided all the errors with which she now reproaches herself, if she had been blessed with a mother such as mine.

LEONORA L—.

THE DUCHESS OF — TO HER DAUGHTER.

MY DEAREST CHILD,

I must answer your last before I sleep—before I can sleep in peace. I have just finished reading the rhapsody which it enclosed; and whilst my mind is full and warm upon the subject, let me write, for I can write to my own satisfaction at no other time. I admire and love you, my child, for the generous indignation you express against those who trample upon the fallen, or who meanly triumph over the errors of superior genius; and if I seem more cold, or more severe, than you wish me to be, attribute this to my anxiety for your happiness, and to that caution which is perhaps the infirmity of age.

In the course of my long life I have, alas! seen vice and folly dressed in so many different fashions, that I can find no difficulty in detecting them under any disguise; but your unpractised eyes are almost as easily deceived as when you were five years old, and when you could not believe that your pasteboard nun was the same person in her various changes of attire.

Nothing would tempt you to associate with those who have avowed themselves regardless of right and wrong; but I must warn you against another, and a far more dangerous class, who professing the most refined delicacy of sentiment, and boasting of invulnerable virtue, exhibit themselves in the most improper and hazardous situations; and who, because they are without fear, expect to be deemed free from reproach. Either from miraculous good fortune, or from a singularity of temper, these adventurous heroines may possibly escape with what they call perfect innocence. So much the worse for society. Their example tempts others, who fall a sacrifice to their weakness and folly. I would punish the tempters in this case more than the victims, and for them the most effectual species of punishment is contempt. Neglect is death to these female lovers of notoriety. The moment they are out of fashion their power to work mischief ceases. Those who from their character and rank have influence over public opinion are bound to consider these things in the choice of their associates. This is peculiarly necessary in days when attempts are made to level all distinctions. You have sometimes hinted to me, my dear daughter, with all proper delicacy, that I am too strict in my notions, and that, unknown to myself, my pride mixes with morality. Be it so: the pride of family, and the pride of virtue, should reciprocally support each other. Were I asked what I think the best guard to a nobility in this or in any other country, I should answer, VIRTUE. I admire that simple epitaph in Westminster Abbey on the Duchess of Newcastle:—"Her name was Margaret Lucas, youngest sister to the Lord Lucas of Colchester;—a noble family, for all the brothers were valiant and all the sisters virtuous."

I look to the temper of the times in forming rules for conduct. Of late years we have seen wonderful changes in female manners. I may be like the old marquis in Gil Blas, who contended that even the peaches of modern days had deteriorated; but I fear that my complaints of the degeneracy of human kind are better founded, than his fears for the vegetable creation. A taste for the elegant profligacy of

French gallantry was, I remember, introduced into this country before the destruction of the French monarchy. Since that time, some sentimental writers and pretended philosophers of our own and foreign countries, have endeavoured to confound all our ideas of morality. To every rule of right they have found exceptions, and on these they have fixed the public attention by adorning them with all the splendid decorations of eloquence; so that the rule is despised or forgotten, and the exception triumphantly established in its stead. These orators seem as if they had been employed by Satan to plead the cause of vice; and, as if possessed by the evil spirit, they speak with a vehemence which carries away their auditors, or with a subtlety which deludes their better judgment. They put extreme cases, in which virtue may become vice, or vice virtue: they exhibit criminal passions in constant connexion with the most exalted, the most amiable virtues; thus making use of the best feelings of human nature for the worst purposes, they engage pity or admiration perpetually on the side of guilt. Eternally talking of philosophy or philanthropy, they borrow the terms only to perplex the ignorant and seduce the imagination. They have their systems and their theories, and in theory they pretend that the general good of society is their sole immutable rule of morality, and in practice they make the variable feelings of each individual the judges of this general good. Their systems disdain all the vulgar virtues, intent upon some beau ideal of perfection or perfectibility. They set common sense and common honesty at defiance. No matter: their doctrine, so convenient to the passions and soporific to the conscience, can never want partisans; especially by weak and enthusiastic women it is adopted and propagated with eagerness; then they become personages of importance, and zealots in support of their sublime opinions; and they can read,—and they can write,—and they can talk,—and they can effect a revolution in public opinion! I am afraid, indeed, that they can; for of late years we have heard more of sentiment than of principles; more of the rights of woman than of her duties. We have seen talents disgraced by the conduct of their possessors, and perverted in the vain attempt to defend what is unjustifiable.

Where must all this end? Where the abuse of reason inevitably ends—in the ultimate law of force. If, in this age of reason, women make a bad use of that power which they have obtained by the cultivation of their understanding, they will degrade and enslave themselves beyond redemption; they will reduce their sex to a situation worse than it ever experienced even in the ages of ignorance and superstition. If men find that the virtue of women diminishes in proportion as intellectual cultivation increases, they will connect, fatally for the freedom and happiness of our sex, the ideas of female ignorance and female innocence; they will decide that one is the effect of the other. They will not pause to distinguish between the use and the abuse of reason; they will not stand by to see further experiments tried at their expense, but they will prohibit knowledge altogether as a pernicious commodity, and will exert the superior power which nature and society place in their hands, to enforce their decrees. Opinion obtained freedom for women; by opinion they may be again enslaved. It is therefore the interest of the female world, and of society, that women should be deterred by the dread of shame from passing the bounds of discretion. No false lenity, no partiality in favour of amusing talents or agreeable manners, should admit of exceptions which become dangerous examples of impunity. The rank and superior understanding of a delinquent ought not to be considered in mitigation, but as aggravating circumstances. Rank makes ill conduct more conspicuous: talents make it more dangerous. Women of abilities, if they err, usually employ all their powers to justify rather than to amend their faults.

I am afraid, my dear daughter, that my general arguments are closing round your Olivia; but I must bid you a good night, for my poor eyes will serve me no longer. God bless you, my dear child.

LEONORA TO HER MOTHER.

I agree with you, my dear mother, that in these times especially it is incumbent upon all persons, whose rank or reputation may influence public opinion, to be particularly careful to support the cause of female honour, of virtue, and religion. With the same object in view, we may however differ in the choice of means for its attainment. Pleasure as well as pain acts upon human creatures; and therefore, in governing them, may not reward be full as efficacious as punishment? Our sex are sufficiently apprised of the fatal consequences of ill conduct; the advantages of well-earned reputation should be at least as great, as certain, and as permanent.

In former times, a single finger pointed at the scutcheon of a knight challenged him to defend his fame; but the defiance was open, the defence was public; and if the charge proved groundless, it injured none but the malicious accuser. In our days, female reputation, which is of a nature more delicate than the honour of any knight, may be destroyed by the finger of private malice. The whisper of secret scandal, which admits of no fair or public answer, is too often sufficient to dishonour a life of spotless fame. This is the height, not only of injustice, but of impolicy. Women will become indifferent to reputation, which it is so difficult, even by the prudence of years, to acquire, and which it is so easy to lose in a moment, by the malice or thoughtlessness of those, who invent, or who repeat scandal. Those who call themselves the world, often judge without listening to evidence, and proceed upon suspicion with as much promptitude and severity, as if they had the most convincing proofs. But because Cæsar, nearly two thousand years ago, said that his wife ought not even to be suspected, and divorced her upon the strength of this sentiment, shall we make it a general maxim that suspicion justifies punishment? We might as well applaud those, who when their friends are barely suspected to be tainted with the plague, drive them from all human comfort and assistance.

Even where women, from the thoughtless gaiety of youth, or the impulse of inexperienced enthusiasm, may have given some slight cause for censure, I would not have virtue put on all her gorgon terrors, nor appear circled by the vengeful band of prudes; her chastening hand will be more beneficially felt if she wear her more benign form. To place the imprudent in the same class with the vicious, is injustice and impolicy; were the same punishment and the same disgrace to be affixed to small and to great offences, the number of capital offenders would certainly increase. Those who were disposed to yield to their passions would, when they had once failed in exact decorum, see no motive, no fear to restrain them; and there would be no pause, no interval between error and profligacy. Amongst females who have been imprudent, there are many things to be considered which ought to recommend them to mercy. The judge, when he is obliged to pronounce the immutable sentence of the law, often, with tears, wishes that it were in his power to mitigate the punishment: the decisions of opinion may and must vary with circumstances, else the degree of reprobation which they inflict cannot be proportioned to the offence, or calculated for the good of society. Among the mitigating circumstances, I should be inclined to name even, those which you bring in aggravation. Talents, and what is called genius, in our sex are often connected with a warmth of heart, an enthusiasm of temper, which expose to dangers, from which the coldness of mediocrity is safe. In the illuminated palace of ice, the lights which render the spectacle splendid, and which raise the admiration of the beholders, endanger the fabric and tend to its destruction.

But you will tell me, dear mother, that allusion is not argument—and I am almost afraid to proceed, lest you should think me an advocate for vice. I would not shut the gates of mercy, inexorably and indiscriminately, upon all those of my own sex, who have even been more than imprudent.

"He taught them shame, the sudden sense of ill—
Shame, Nature's hasty conscience, which forbids
Weak inclination ere it grows to will,
Or stays rash will before it grows to deeds."

Whilst a woman is alive to shame she cannot be dead to virtue. But by injudicious or incessant reproach, this principle, even where it is most exquisite, may be most easily destroyed. The mimosa, when too long exposed to each rude touch, loses its retractile sensibility. It ought surely to be the care of the wise and benevolent to cherish that principle, implanted in our nature as the guard of virtue, that principle, upon which legislators rest the force of punishment, and all the grand interests of society.

My dear mother, perhaps you will be surprised at the style in which I have been writing, and you will smile at hearing your Leonora discuss the duties of legislators and the grand interests of society. She has not done so from presumption, or from affectation. She was alarmed by your supposing that her judgment was deluded by fascinating manners, and she determined to produce general arguments, to convince you that she is not actuated by particular prepossession. You see that I have at least some show of reason on my side. I have forborne to mention Olivia's name: but now that I have obviated, I hope by reasoning, the imputation of partiality, I may observe that all my arguments are strongly in her favour. She had been attacked by slander; the world has condemned her upon suspicion merely. She has been imprudent; but I repeat, in the strongest terms, that I am convinced of her innocence; and that I should bitterly regret that a woman with such an affectionate heart, such uncommon candour, and such superior abilities, should be lost to society.

Tell me, my dear mother, that you are no longer in anxiety about the consequences of my attachment to Olivia.

Your affectionate daughter,

LEONORA.

LETTER VI

THE DUCHESS OF — TO HER DAUGHTER.

You lament, my dear child, that such an affectionate heart, such great abilities as Olivia's, should be lost to society. Before I sympathize in your pity, my judgment must be convinced that it is reasonable.

What proofs has Lady Olivia given of her affectionate heart? She is at variance with both her parents; she is separated from her husband; and she leaves her child in a foreign country, to be educated by strangers. Am I to understand, that her ladyship's neglecting to perform the duties of a daughter, a wife, and a mother, are proofs of an affectionate heart? As to her superior talents, do they contribute to her own happiness, or to the happiness of others? Evidently not to her own; for by her account of herself, she is one of the most miserable wretches alive! She tells you that "she went to foreign climes in search of balm for a wounded heart, and wandered from place to place, looking for what no place could afford." She talks of "indescribable sadness—an aching void—an impenetrable prison—darkness visible—dead bodies chained to living ones;" and she exhibits all the disordered furniture of a "diseased mind." But you say, that though her powers are thus insufficient to make herself happy, they may amuse or instruct the world; and of this I am to judge by the letters which you have sent me. You admire fine writing; so do I. I class eloquence high amongst the fine arts. But by eloquence I mean something more than Dr. Johnson defines it to be, "the art of speaking with fluency and elegance." This is an art which is now possessed to a certain degree by every boarding-school miss. Every scribbling young lady can now string sentences and sentiments together, and can turn a period harmoniously. Upon the strength of these accomplishments they commence heroines, and claim the privileges of the order; privileges which go to an indefinite and most alarming extent. Every heroine may have her own code of morality for her private use, and she is to be tried by no other; she may rail as loudly as she pleases "at the barbarous institutions of society," and may deplore "the inexorable tyranny of the English laws." If she find herself involved in delicate entanglements of crossing duties, she may break through any one, or all of them, to extricate herself with a noble contempt of prejudice.

I have promised to reason calmly; but I cannot repress the terror which I feel at the idea of my daughter's becoming the friend of one of these women. Olivia's letters are, I think, in the true heroine style; and they might make a brilliant figure in a certain class of novels. She begins with a bold exclamation on "the misfortune of being born a woman!—the slave or the outcast of society, condemned to incessant hypocrisy!" Does she mean modesty? Her manly soul feels it "the most degrading punishment that omnipotent cruelty could devise, to be imprisoned in a female form." From such a masculine spirit some fortitude and magnanimity might be expected; but presently she begs to be pitied, for a broken spirit, and more than female tenderness of heart. I have observed that the ladies who wish to be men, are usually those who have not sufficient strength of mind to be women.

Olivia proceeds in an ironical strain to envy, as "the happiest of their sex, those who submit to be swathed by custom." These persons she stigmatizes with the epithet of tideless-blooded. It is the common trick of unprincipled women to affect to despise those who conduct themselves with propriety. Prudence they term coldness; fortitude, insensibility; and regard to the rights of others, prejudice. By this perversion of terms they would laugh or sneer virtue out of countenance; and, by robbing her of all praise, they would deprive her of all immediate motive. Conscious of their own degradation, they would lower every thing, and every body, to their own standard: they would make you believe, that those who have not yielded to their passions are destitute of sensibility; that the love which is not blazoned forth in glaring colours is not entitled to our sympathy. The sacrifice of the strongest feelings of the human heart to a sense of duty is to be called mean, or absurd; but the shameless frenzy of passion, exposing itself to public gaze, is to be an object of admiration. These heroines talk of strength of mind; but they forget that strength of mind is to be shown in resisting their passions, not in yielding to them. Without being absolutely of an opinion, which I have heard maintained, that all virtue is sacrifice, I am convinced that the essential characteristic of virtue is to bear and forbear. These sentimentalists can do neither. They talk of sacrifices and generosity; but they are the veriest egotists—the most selfish creatures alive.

Open your eyes, my dear Leonora, and see things as they really are. Lady Olivia thinks it a sufficient excuse for abandoning her husband, to say, that she found "his soul was not in unison with hers." She thinks it an adequate apology for a criminal attachment, to tell you that "the net was thrown over her heart before she felt her danger: that all its struggles were to no purpose, but to exhaust her strength."

If she did not feel her danger, she prepared it. The course of reading which her ladyship followed was the certain preparation for her subsequent conduct. She tells us that she could not endure "the common-place of morality, but metaphysics promised her some relief." In these days a heroine need not be amoralist, but she must be a metaphysician. She must "wander in the not inelegant labyrinth;" and if in the midst of it she comes unawares upon the monster vice, she must not start, though she have no clue to secure her retreat.

From metaphysics Lady Olivia went on to German novels. "For her largest portions of bliss, for those rapt moments, which consigned vulgar realities to oblivion," she owns herself indebted to those writers, who promise an ideal world of pleasure, which, like the mirage in the desert, bewilders the feverish imagination. I always suspected the imagination of these women of feeling to be more susceptible than their hearts. They want excitation for their morbid sensibility, and they care not at what expense it is procured. If they could make all the pleasures of life into one cordial, they would swallow it at a draught in a fit of sentimental spleen. The mental intemperance that they indulge in promiscuous novel-reading destroys all vigour and clearness of judgment; every thing dances in the varying medium of their imagination. Sophistry passes for reasoning; nothing appears profound but what is obscure; nothing sublime but what is beyond the reach of mortal comprehension. To their vitiated taste the simple pathos, which o'ersteps not the modesty of nature, appears cold, tame, and insipid; they must have scenes and a coup de theatre; and ranting, and raving, and stabbing, and drowning, and poisoning; for with them there is no love without murder. Love, in their representations, is indeed a distorted, ridiculous, horrid monster, from whom common sense, taste, decency, and nature recoil.

But I will be calm.—You say, my dear Leonora, that your judgment has not been blinded by Lady Olivia's fascinating manners; but that you are strongly influenced in her favour by that candour, with which she has revealed to you all her faults. The value of candour in individuals should be measured by their sensibility to shame. When a woman throws off all restraint, and then desires me to admire her candour, I am astonished only at her assurance. Do not be the dupe of such candour. Lady Olivia avows a criminal passion, yet you say that you have no doubt of her innocence. The persuasion of your unsuspecting heart is no argument: when you give me any proofs in her favour, I shall pay them all due attention. In the mean time I have given you my opinion of those ladies who place themselves in the most perilous situations, and then expect you to believe them safe.

Olivia's professions of regard for you are indeed enthusiastic. She tells you, that "your power is unlimited over her heart and understanding; that your friendship would be to her one of the greatest of earthly blessings." May be so—but I cannot wish you to be her friend. With whatever confidence she makes the assertion, do not believe that she has a heart capable of feeling the value of yours. These sentimental, unprincipled women make the worst friends in the world. We are often told that, "poor creatures! they do nobody any harm but themselves;" but in society it is scarcely possible for a woman to do harm to herself, without doing harm to others; all her connexions must be involved in the consequences of her imprudence. Besides, what confidence can you repose in them? If you should happen to be an obstacle in the way of any of their fancies, do you think that they will respect you or your interest, when they have not scrupled to sacrifice their own to the gratification of their passions? Do you think that the gossamer of sentiment will restrain those whom the strong chains of prudence could not hold?

Oh! my dearest child, forcibly as these arguments carry conviction to my mind, I dread lest your compassionate, generous temper, should prevent their reaching your understanding. Then let me conjure you, by all the respect which you have ever shown for your mother's opinions, by all that you hold dear or sacred, beware of forming an intimacy with an unprincipled woman. Believe me to be

Your truly affectionate mother,

LETTER VII

LEONORA TO HER MOTHER.

No daughter ever felt more respect for the opinions of a parent than I do for yours, my dearest mother; but you have never, even from childhood, required from me a blind submission—you have always encouraged me to desire conviction. And now, when the happiness of another is at stake, you will forgive me if I am less disposed to yield than I should be, I hope, if my own interest or taste were alone concerned.

You ask me what proofs I have of Lady Olivia's innocence. Believe me, I have such as are convincing to my unbiassed judgment, and such as would be sufficient to satisfy all your doubts, were I at liberty to lay the whole truth before you. But even to exculpate herself, Olivia will not ruin in your opinion her husband, of whom you imagine that she has no reason to complain. I, who know how anxious she is to obtain your esteem, can appreciate the sacrifice that she makes; and in this instance, as in many others, I admire her magnanimity; it is equal to her candour, for which she is entitled to praise even by your own principles, dear mother: since, far from having thrown off all restraint, she is exquisitely susceptible of shame.

As to her understanding—have no persons of great talents ever been unfortunate? Frequently we see that they have not been able, by all their efforts and all their powers, to remedy the defects in the characters and tempers of those with whom they have unhappily been connected. Olivia married very young, and was unfortunately mistaken in her choice of a husband: on that subject I can only deplore her error and its consequences: but as to her disagreements with her own family, I do not think her to blame. For the mistakes we make in the choice of lovers or friends we may be answerable, but we cannot be responsible for the faults of the relations who are given to us by nature. If we do not please them, it may be our misfortune; it is not necessarily our fault. I cannot be more explicit, without betraying Lady Olivia's confidence, and implicating others in defending her.

With respect to that attachment of which you speak with so much just severity, she has given me the strongest assurances that she will do every thing in her power to conquer it. Absence, you know, is the first and the most difficult step, and this she has taken. Her course of reading displeases you: I cannot defend it: but I am persuaded that it is not a proof of her taste being vitiated. Many people read ordinary novels as others take snuff, merely from habit, from the want of petty excitation; and not, as you suppose, from the want of exorbitant or improper stimulus. Those who are unhappy have recourse to any trifling amusement that can change the course of their thoughts. I do not justify Olivia for having chosen such comforters as certain novels, but I pity her, and impute this choice to want of fortitude, not to depravity of taste. Before she married, a strict injunction was laid upon her not to read any book that was called a novel: this raised in her mind a sort of perverse curiosity. By making any books or opinions contraband, the desire to read and circulate them is increased; bad principles are consequently smuggled into families, and being kept secret, can never be subject to fair examination. I think it must be advantageous to the right side of any question, that all which can be said against it should be openly heard, that it may be answered. I do not

"Hate when vice can bolt her arguments;"

for I know that virtue has a tongue to answer her. The more vice repeats her assertions, the better; because when familiarized, their boldness will not astound the understanding, and the charm of novelty will not be mistaken for the power of truth. We may observe, that the admiration for the class of writers to whom you allude, though violent in its commencement, has abated since they have been more known; and numbers, who began with rapture, have ended with disgust. Persons of vivacious imaginations, like Olivia, may be caught at first view by whatever has the appearance of grandeur or sublimity; but if time be allowed for examination, they will infallibly detect the disproportions, and these will ever afterwards shock their taste: if you will not allow leisure for comparison—if you say, do not look at such strange objects, the obedient eyes may turn aside, but the rebel imagination pictures something a thousand times more wonderful and charming than the reality. I will venture to predict, that Olivia will soon be tired of the species of novels which she now admires, and that, once surfeited with these books, and convinced of their pernicious effects, she will never relapse into the practice of novel reading.

As to her taste for metaphysical books—Dear mother, I am very daring to differ with you in so many points; but permit me to say, that I do not agree with you in detesting metaphysics. People may lose themselves in that labyrinth; but why should they meet with vice in the midst of it? The characters of a moralist, a practical moralist, and a metaphysician, are not incompatible, as we may see in many amiable and illustrious examples. To examine human motives, and the nature of the human mind, is not to destroy the power of virtue, or to increase the influence of vice. The chemist, after analyzing certain substances, and after discovering their constituent parts, can lay aside all that is heterogeneous, and recompound the substance in a purer state. From analogy we might infer, that the motives of metaphysicians ought to be purer than those of the vulgar and ignorant. To discover the art of converting base into noble passions, or to obtain a universal remedy for all mental diseases, is perhaps beyond the power of metaphysicians; but in the pursuit, useful discoveries may be made.

As to Olivia's letters—I am sorry I sent them to you; for I see that they have lowered, instead of raising her in your opinion. But if you criticise letters, written in openness and confidence of heart to a private friend, as if they were set before the tribunal of the public, you are—may I say it?—not only severe, but unjust; for you try and condemn the subjects of one country by the laws of another.

Dearest mother, be half as indulgent to Olivia as you are to me: indeed you are prejudiced against her; and because you see some faults, you think her whole character vicious. But would you cut down a fine tree because a leaf is withered, or because the canker-worm has eaten into the bud? Even if a main branch were decayed, are there not remedies which, skilfully applied, can save the tree from destruction, and perhaps restore it to its pristine beauty?

And now, having exhausted all my allusions, all my arguments, and all my little stock of eloquence, I must come to a plain matter of fact—

Before I received your letter I had invited Lady Olivia to spend some time at L— Castle. I fear that you will blame my precipitation, and I reproach myself for it, because I know it will give you pain. However, though you will think me imprudent, I am certain you would rather that I were imprudent than unjust. I have defended Olivia from what I believe to be unmerited censure; I have invited her to my house; she has accepted my proffered kindness; to withdraw it afterwards would be doing her irreparable injury: it would confirm all that the world can suspect: it would be saying to the censorious—I am convinced that you are right, and I deliver your victim up to you.

Thus I should betray the person whom I undertook to defend: her confidence in me, her having but for a moment accepted my protection, would be her ruin. I could not act in so base a manner.

Fear nothing for me, my best, but too anxious, friend. I may do Lady Olivia some good; she can do me no harm. She may learn the principles which you have taught me; I can never catch from her any tastes or habits which you would disapprove. As to the rest, I hazard little or nothing. The hereditary credit which I enjoy in my maternal right enables me to assist others without injuring myself.

Your affectionate daughter,

LEONORA.

LETTER VIII

THE DUCHESS OF — TO HER DAUGHTER.

MY DEAREST CHILD,

I hope that you are in the right, and that I am in the wrong.

Your affectionate mother,

LETTER IX

OLIVIA TO MADAME DE P—.

Prepare yourself, my ever dear and charming Gabrielle, for all the torments of jealousy. Know, that since I came to England I have formed a new friendship with a woman who is interesting in the extreme, who has charmed me by the simplicity of her manners and the generous sensibility of her heart. Her character is certainly too reserved: yet even this defect has perhaps increased her power over my imagination, and consequently over my affections. I know not by what magic she has obtained it, but she has already an ascendancy over me, which would quite astonish you, who know my wayward fancies and independent spirit.

Alas! I confess my heart is weak indeed; and I fear that all the power of friendship and philosophy combined will never strengthen it sufficiently. Oh, Gabrielle! how can I hope to obliterate from my soul that attachment which has marked the colour of my destiny for years? Yet such courage, such cruel courage is required of me, and of such I have boasted myself capable. Lady Leonora L—, my new friend, has, by all the English eloquence of virtue, obtained from me a promise, which, I fear, I shall not have the fortitude to keep—but I must make the attempt—Forbid R— to write to me—Yes! I have written the words—Forbid R— to write to me—Forbid him to think of me—I will do more—if possible I will forbid myself henceforward to think of him—to think of love—Adieu, my Gabrielle—All the illusions of life are over, and a dreary blank of future existence lies before me, terminated only by the grave. To-morrow I go to L— Castle, with feelings which I can compare only to those of the unfortunate La Valliere when she renounced her lover, and resolved to bury herself in a cloister.—Alas! why have not I the resource of devotion?

Your unhappy

OLIVIA.

LETTER X

GENERAL B— TO MR. L—.

Publish my travels!—Not I, my dear friend. The world shall never have the pleasure of laughing at General B—'s trip to Paris. Before a man sets about to inform others, he should have seen, not only the surface but the bottom of things; he should have had, not only a vue d'oiseau, but (to use a celebrated naval commander's expression) a vue de poisson of his subject. By this time you must have heard enough of the Louvre and the Tuilleries, and Versailles, and le petit Trianon, and St. Cloud—and you have had enough of pictures and statues; and you know all that can be known of Bonaparte, by seeing him at a review or a levee; and the fashionable beauties and celebrated characters of the hour have all passed and repassed through the magic lantern. A fresh showman might make his figures a little more correct, or a little more in laughable caricature, but he could produce nothing new. Alas! there is nothing new under the sun. Nothing remains for the moderns, but to practise the oldest follies the newest ways. Would you, for the sake of your female friends, know the fashionable dress of a Parisian elegante, see Seneca on the transparent vestments of the Roman ladies, who, like these modern belles, were generous in the display of their charms to the public. No doubt these French republicanists act upon the true Spartan principle of modesty: they take the most efficacious method to prevent their influence from being too great over the imaginations of men, by renouncing all that insidious reserve which alone can render even beauty permanently dangerous.

Of the cruelties of the revolution I can tell you nothing new. The public have been steeped up to the lips in blood, and have surely had their fill of horrors.

But, my dear friend, you say that I must be able to give a just view of the present state of French society, and of the best parts of it, because I have not, like some of my countrymen, hurried about Paris from one spectacle to another, seen the opera, and the play-houses, and the masked balls, and the gaming-houses, and the women of the Palais Royal, and the lions of all sorts; gone through the usual routine of presentation and public dinners, drunk French wine, damned French cookery, and "come home content." I have certainly endeavoured to employ my time better, and have had the good fortune to be admitted into the best private societies in Paris. These were composed of the remains of the French nobility, of men of letters and science, and of families, who, without interfering in politics, devote themselves to domestic duties, to literary and social pleasures. The happy hours I have passed in this society can never be forgotten, and the kindness I have received has made its full impression upon an honest English heart. I will never disgrace the confidence of my friends, by drawing their characters for the public.

Cæsar in all his glory, and all his despotism, could not, with impunity, force a Roman knight [*] to go upon the stage: but modern anecdote-mongers, more cruel and insolent than Cæsar, force their friends of all ages and sexes to appear, and speak, and act, for the amusement or derision of the public.

[*Laberius.]

My dear friend, is not my resolution, never to favour the world with my tour, well grounded? I hope that I have proved to your satisfaction, that I could tell people nothing but what I do not understand, or what is not worth telling them, or what has been told them a hundred times, or what, as a gentleman, I am bound not to publish.

Yours truly,

J. B.

OLIVIA TO MADAME DE P—.

L— Castle.

Friendship, my amiable and interesting Gabrielle, is more an affair of the heart than of the head, more the instinct of taste than the choice of reason. With me the heart is no longer touched, when the imagination ceases to be charmed. Explain to me this metaphysical phenomenon of my nature, and, for your reward, I will quiet your jealousy, by confessing without compunction what now weighs on my conscience terribly. I begin to feel that I can never love this English friend as I ought. She is too English— far too English for one who has known the charms of French ease, vivacity, and sentiment; for one who has seen the bewitching Gabrielle's infinite variety.

Leonora has just the figure and face that you would picture to yourself for une belle Anglaise; and if our Milton comes into your memory, you might repeat, for the quotation is not too trite for a foreigner,

"Grace is in all her steps, heaven in her eye, In every gesture dignity and love."

But then it is grace which says nothing, a heaven only for a husband, the dignity more of a matron than of a heroine, and love that might have suited Eve before she had seen this world. Leonora is certainly a beauty; but then a beauty who does not know her power, and who, consequently, can make no one else feel its full extent. She is not unlike your beautiful Polish Princess, but she has none of the charming Anastasia's irresistible transitions from soft, silent languor, to brilliant, eloquent enthusiasm. All the gestures and attitudes of Anastasia are those of taste and sentiment; Leonora's are simply those of nature. La belle nature, but not le beau ideal. With a figure that would grace any court, or shine upon any stage, she usually enters a room without producing, or thinking of producing, any sensation; she moves often without seeming to have any other intention than to change her place; and her fine eyes generally look as if they were made only to see with. At times she certainly has a most expressive and intelligent countenance. I have seen her face enlightened by the fire of genius, and shaded by the exquisite touches of sensibility; but all this is merely called forth by the occasion, and vanishes before it is noticed by half the company. Indeed, the full radiance of her beauty or of her wit seldom shines upon any one but her husband. The audience and spectators are forgotten. Heavens! what a difference between the effect which Leonora and Gabrielle produce! But, to do her justice, much of this arises from the different organization of French and English society. In Paris the insipid details of domestic life are judiciously kept behind the scenes, and women appear as heroines upon the stage with all the advantages of decoration, to listen to the language of love, and to receive the homage of public admiration. In England, gallantry is not yet systematized, and our sex look more to their families than to what is called society for the happiness of existence. And yet the affection of mothers for their children does not appear to be so strong in the hearts of English as of French women. In England, ladies do not talk of the sentiment of maternity with that elegance and sensibility with which you expatiate upon it continually in conversation. They literally are des bonnes meres de famille, not from the impulse of sentiment, but merely from an early instilled sense of duty, for which they deserve little credit. However, they devote their lives to their children, and those who have the misfortune to be their intimate friends are doomed to see them half the day, or all day long, go through the part of the good mother in all its diurnal monotony of lessons and caresses. All this may be vastly right—it is a pity it is so tiresome. For my part I cannot conceive how persons of superior taste and talents can submit to it, unless it be to make themselves a reputation, and that you know is done by writing and talking on the general principles, not by submitting to the minute details of education. The great painter sketches the outline, and touches the principal features, but leaves the subordinate drudgery of filling up the parts, finishing the drapery, &c., to inferior hands.

Upon recollection, in my favourite "Sorrows of Werter," the heroine is represented cutting bread and butter for a group of children: I admire this simplicity in Goethe; 'tis one of the secrets by which he touches the heart. Simplicity is delightful by way of variety, but always simplicity is worse than toujours perdrix. Children in a novel or a drama are charming little creatures: but in real life they are often insufferable plagues. What becomes of them in Paris I know not; but I am sure that they are never in the way of one's conversations or reveries; and it would be a blessing to society if English children were as inaudible and invisible. These things strike me sensibly upon my return to England, after so long an absence. Surely, by means of the machinery of masters, and governesses, and schools, the manufacture of education might be carried on without incommoding those who desire to see only the finished production. Here I find the daughter of an English duke, a woman in the first bloom of youth, of the highest pretensions in point of rank, beauty, fashion, accomplishments, and talents, devoting herself to the education of two children, orphans, left to her care by an elder sister. To take charge of orphans is a good and fine action; as such it touches me sensibly; but then where is the necessity of sacrificing one's friends, and one's pleasures, day after day, and hour after hour, to mere children? Leonora can persevere only from a notion of duty. Now, in my opinion, when generosity becomes duty it ceases to be virtue. Virtue requires free-will: duty implies constraint. Virtue acts from the impulse of the moment, and never tires or is tired; duty drudges on in consequence of reflection, and, weary herself, wearies all beholders. Duty, always laborious, never can be graceful; and what is not graceful in woman cannot be amiable—can it, my amiable Gabrielle? But I reproach myself for all I have written. Leonora is my friend—besides, I am really obliged to her, and for the universe would I not hint a thought to her disadvantage. Indeed she is a most excellent, a faultless character, and it is the misfortune of your Olivia not to love perfection as she ought.

My charming and interesting Gabrielle, I am more out of humour with myself than you can conceive; for in spite of all that reason and gratitude urge, I fear I cannot prefer the insipid virtues of Leonora to the lively graces of Gabrielle.

As to the cold husband, Mr. L—, I neither know nor wish to know any thing of him; but I live in hopes of an agreeable and interesting accession to our society to-day, from the arrival of Leonora's intimate friend, a young widow, whose husband I understand was a man of a harsh temper: she has gone through severe trials with surprising fortitude; and though I do not know her history, I am persuaded it must be interesting. Assuredly this husband could never have been the man of her choice, and of course she must have had some secret unhappy attachment, which doubtless preyed upon her spirits. Probably the object of her affection, in despair at her marriage, plighted his faith unfortunately, or possibly may have fallen a sacrifice to his constancy. I am all impatience to see her. Her husband's name was so ruggedly English, that I am sure you would never be able to pronounce it, especially if you only saw it written; therefore I shall always to you call her Helen, a name which is more pleasing to the ear, and more promising to the imagination. I have not been able to prevail upon Leonora to describe her friend to me exactly; she says only, that she loves Helen too well to overpraise her beforehand. My busy fancy has, however, bodied forth her form, and painted her in the most amiable and enchanting colours. Hark! she is just arrived. Adieu.

OLIVIA.

LETTER XII

FROM MRS. C— TO MISS B—.

. . . Having now had the honour of spending nearly a week in the society of the celebrated enchantress, Lady Olivia, you will naturally expect that I should be much improved in the art of love: but before I come to my improvements I must tell you, what will be rather more interesting, that Leonora is perfectly well and happy, and that I have the dear delight of exclaiming ten times an hour, "Ay, just as I thought it would be!—Just such a wife, just such a mistress of a family I knew she would make."

"Not to admire," is an art or a precept which I have not been able to practise much since I came here. Some philosophers tell us that admiration is not only a silly but a fatiguing state of mind; and I suppose that nothing could have preserved my mind from being tired to death, but the quantity of bodily exercise which I have taken. I could, if I pleased, give you a plan and elevation of this castle. Nay, I doubt not but I could stand an examination in the catalogue of the pictures, or the inventory of the furniture.

You, Helen!—you who could not remember the colour of Lady N—'s new curtains after you had seen them at least a hundred times!

Lady N— was indifferent to me, and how could I hang up her curtains in my memory? By what could they hold? Do you not know, Margaret ... all the fine things that I could say, and that quartos have said before me, about the association of ideas and sensations, &c.? Those we love impart to uninteresting objects the power of pleasing, as the magnet can communicate to inert metal its attractive influence.

Till Mr. L— was Leonora's lover I never liked him much. I do not mean to call him inert. I always knew that he had many excellent qualities; but there was nothing in his temper peculiarly agreeable to me, and there was something in his character that I did not thoroughly understand; yet, since he is become Leonora's husband, I find my understanding much improved, and I dare say it will soon be so far enlarged, that I shall comprehend him perfectly.

Leonora has almost persuaded me to like Lady Olivia. Not to laugh at her would be impossible. I wish you could see the way in which we go on together. Our first setting out would have diverted you. Enter Lady Olivia breathless, with an air of theatric expectation—advances to embrace Helen, who is laughing with Leonora—her back turned towards the side of the stage at which Olivia enters—Olivia pauses suddenly, and measures Helen with a long look. What passes in Lady Olivia's mind at this moment I do not know, but I guess that she was disappointed woefully by my appearance. After some time she was recovered, by Leonora's assistance, from her reverie, and presently began to admire my vivacity, and to find out that I was Clarissa's Miss Howe—no, I was Lady G.—no, I was Heloise's Clara: but I, choosing to be myself, and insisting upon being an original, sunk again visibly and rapidly in Olivia's opinion, till I was in imminent danger of being nobody, Leonora again kindly interposed to save me from annihilation; and after an interval of an hour or two dedicated to letter-writing, Lady Olivia returned and seated herself beside me, resolved to decide what manner of woman I was. Certain novels are the touchstones of feeling and intellect with certain ladies. Unluckily I was not well read in these; and in the questions put to me from these sentimental statute-books, I gave strange judgments, often for the husband or parents against the heroine. I did not even admit the plea of destiny, irresistible passion, or entrancement, as in all cases sufficient excuse for all errors and crimes. Moreover, I excited astonishment by calling things by obsolete names. I called a married woman's having a lover a crime! Then I was no judge of virtues, for I thought a wife's making an intimate friend of her husband's mistress was scandalous and mean; but this I was told is the height of delicacy and generosity. I could not perceive the propriety of a man's liking two women at the same time, or a woman's having a platonic attachment for half a dozen lovers: and I owned that I did not wish divorce could be as easily obtained in England as in France. All which proved that I have never been out of England—a great misfortune! I dare say it will soon be discovered that women as well as madeira cannot be good for any thing till they have crossed the line. But besides the obloquy of having lived only in the best company in England, I was further disgraced by the discovery, that I am deplorably ignorant of metaphysics, and have never been enlightened by any philanthropic transcendental foreign professor of humanity. Profoundly humiliated, and not having yet taken the first step towards knowledge, the knowing that I was ignorant, I was pondering upon my sad fate, when Lady Olivia, putting her hand upon my shoulder, summoned me into the court of love, there in my own proper person to answer such questions as it should please her ladyship to ask. For instance:—"Were you ever in love?—How often?—When?—Where?—And with whom?"

Never having stood a cross-examination in public upon these points, I was not quite prepared to reply; and I was accused of giving evasive answers, and convicted of blushing. Mr. L—, who was present at this examination, enjoyed, in his grave way, my astonishment and confusion, but said not one word. I rallied my spirits and my wits, and gave some answers which gained the smile of the court on my side.

From these specimens you may guess, my dear Margaret, how well this lady and I are likely to agree. I shall divert myself with her absurdities without scruple. Yet notwithstanding the flagrancy of these, Leonora persuades me to think well of Olivia; indeed I am so happy here, that it would be a difficult matter at present to make me think ill of any body. The good qualities, which Leonora sees in her, are not yet visible to my eyes; but Leonora's visual orb is so cleared with charity and love, that she can discern what is not revealed to vulgar sight. Even in the very germ, she discovers the minute form of the perfect flower. The Olivia will, I hope, in time, blow out in full perfection.

Yours affectionately,

HELEN C—.

OLIVIA TO MADAME DE P—.

Monday.

O my Gabrielle! this Helen is not precisely the person that I expected. Instead of being a dejected beauty, she is all life and gaiety.

I own I should like her better if she were a little more pensive; a tinge of melancholy would, in her situation, be so becoming and natural. My imagination was quite disappointed when I beheld the quickness of her eyes and frequency of her smiles. Even her mode of showing affection to Leonora was not such as could please me. This is the first visit, I understand, that she has paid Leonora since her marriage: these friends have been separated for many months.—I was not present at their meeting; but I came into the room a few minutes after Helen's arrival, and I should have thought that they had seen one another but yesterday. This dear Helen was quite at ease and at home in a few moments, and seemed as if she had been living with us for years. I make allowance for the ease of well-bred people. Helen has lived much in the world, and has polished manners. But the heart—the heart is superior to politeness; and even ease, in some situations, shows a want of the delicate tact of sentiment. In a similar situation I should have been silent, entranced, absorbed in my sensations—overcome by them, perhaps dissolved in tears. But in Helen there appeared no symptoms of real sensibility—nothing characteristic—nothing profound—nothing concentrated: it was all superficial, and evaporated in the common way. I was provoked to see Leonora satisfied. She assures me that Helen has uncommonly strong affections, and that her character rather exceeds than is deficient in enthusiasm. Possibly; but I am certain that Helen is in no danger of becoming romantic. Far from being abstracted, I never saw any one seem more interested and eager about every present occurrence—pleased, even to childishness, with every passing trifle. I confess that she is too much of this world for me. But I will if possible suspend my judgment, and study her a few hours longer, before I give you my definitive opinion.

Thursday.

Well, my Gabrielle, my definitive opinion is that I can never love this friend of Leonora. I said that she had lived much in the world—but only in the English world: she has never seen any other; therefore, though quite in a different style from Leonora, she shocks me with the same nationality. All her ideas are exclusively English: she has what is called English good sense, and English humour, and English prejudices of all sorts, both masculine and feminine. She takes fire in defence of her country and of her sex; nay, sometimes blushes even to awkwardness, which one would not expect in the midst of her good breeding and vivacity. What a difference between her vivacity and that of my charming Gabrielle! as great as between the enlargement of your mind and the limited nature of her understanding. I tried her on various subjects, but found her intrenched in her own contracted notions. All new, or liberal, or sublime ideas in morality or metaphysics she either cannot seize, or seizes only to place in a ridiculous point of view: a certain sign of mediocrity. Adieu, my Gabrielle. I must send you the pictures, whether engaging or forbidding, of those with whom your Olivia is destined to pass her time. When I have no events to relate, still I must write to convey to you my sentiments. Alas! how imperfectly!—for I have interdicted myself the expression of those most interesting to my heart. Leonora, calmly prudent, coolly virtuous, knows not what it costs me to be faithful to this cruel promise. Write to me, my sympathizing, my tender friend!

Your ever unhappy

OLIVIA.

LETTER XIV

MRS. C— TO MISS B—.

July 10th.

Some very good people, like some very fine pictures, are best at a distance. But Leonora is not one of these: the nearer you approach, the better you like her; as in arabesque-work you may admire the beauty of the design even at a distance, but you cannot appreciate the delicacy of the execution till you examine it closely, and discover that every line is formed of grains of gold, almost imperceptibly fine. I am glad that the "small sweet courtesies of life" have been hailed by one sentimental writer at least. The minor virtues are not to be despised, even in comparison with the most exalted. The common rose, I have often thought, need not be ashamed of itself even in company with the finest exotics in a hothouse; and I remember, that your brother, in one of his letters, observed, that the common cock makes a very respectable figure, even in the grand Parisian assembly of all the stuffed birds and beasts in the universe. It is a glorious thing to have a friend who will jump into a river, or down a precipice, to save one's life: but as I do not intend to tumble down precipices, or to throw myself into the water above half a dozen times, I would rather have for my friends persons who would not reserve their kindness wholly for these grand occasions, but who could condescend to make me happy every day, and all day long, even by actions not sufficiently sublime to be recorded in history or romance.

Do not infer from this that I think Leonora would hesitate to make great sacrifices. I have had sufficient experience of her fortitude and active courage of mind in the most trying circumstances, whilst many who talked more stoutly, shrunk from committing themselves by actions.

Some maxim-maker says, that past misfortunes are good for nothing but to be forgotten. I am not of his opinion: I think that they are good to make us know our winter from our summer friends, and to make us feel for those who have sustained us in adversity, that most pleasurable sensation of the human mind—gratitude.

But I am straying unawares into the province of sentiment, where I am such a stranger that I shall inevitably lose my way, especially as I am too proud to take a guide. Lady Olivia — may perhaps be very fond of Leonora: and as she has every possible cause to be so, it is but reasonable and charitable to suppose that she is: but I should never guess it by her manner. She speaks of her friendship sometimes in the most romantic style, but often makes observations upon the enviable coolness and imperturbability of Leonora's disposition, which convinces me that she does not understand it in the least. Those who do not really feel, always pitch their expressions too high or too low, as deaf people bellow, or speak in a whisper. But I may be mistaken in my suspicions of Olivia; for to do the lady justice, as Mrs. Candour would say, she is so affected, that it is difficult to know what she really feels. Those who put on rouge occasionally, are suspected of wearing it constantly, and never have any credit for their natural colour; presently they become so accustomed to common rouge, that, mistaking scarlet for pale pink, they persist in laying on more and more, till they are like nothing human.

Yours affectionately,

HELEN C—.

LETTER XV

OLIVIA TO MADAME DE P—.

I have found it! I have found it! dear Gabrielle, rejoice with me! I have solved the metaphysical problem, which perplexed me so cruelly, and now I am once more at peace with myself. I have discovered the reason why I cannot love Leonora as she merits to be loved—she has obliged me; and the nature of obligation is such, that it supposes superiority on one side, and consequently destroys the equality, the freedom, the ease, the charm of friendship. Gratitude weighs upon one's heart in proportion to the delicacy of its feelings. To minds of an ordinary sort it may be pleasurable, for with them it is sufficiently feeble to be calm; but in souls of a superior cast, it is a poignant, painful sensation, because it is too strong ever to be tranquil. In short,

"'Tis bliss but to a certain bound—

Beyond, 'tis agony."

For my own part, the very dread that I shall not be thought to express enough, deprives me of the power to speak or even to feel. Fear, you know, extinguishes affection; and of all fears, the dread of not being sufficiently grateful, operates the most powerfully. Thus sensibility destroys itself.—Gracious Heaven! teach me to moderate mine.

In the nature of the obligation with which Leonora has oppressed my heart, there is something peculiarly humiliating. Upon my return to this country, I found the malignant genius of scandal bent upon destroying my reputation. You have no idea of the miserable force of prejudice which still prevails here. There are some women who emancipate themselves, but then unluckily they are not in sufficient numbers to keep each other in countenance in public. One would not choose to be confined to the society of people who cannot go to court, though sometimes they take the lead elsewhere. We are full half a century behind you in civilization; and your revolution has, I find, afforded all our stiffened moralists incontrovertible arguments against liberty of opinion or conduct in either sex.

I was thunderstruck when I saw the grave and repulsive faces of all my female acquaintance. At first I attributed every thing that was strange and disagreeable to English reserve, of which I had retained a sufficiently formidable idea: but I presently found that there was some other cause which kept all these nice consciences at a distance from my atmosphere.

Would you believe it? I saw myself upon the point of being quite excluded from good society. Leonora saved me from this imminent danger. Voluntarily, and I must say nobly, if not gracefully, Leonora came forward in my defence. Vanquishing her natural English timidity, she braved the eyes, and tongues, and advice of all the prudes and old dowagers my enemies, amongst whom I may count the superannuated Duchess her mother, the proudest dowager now living. When I appeared in public with a personage of Leonora's unblemished reputation, scandal, much against her will, was forced to be silent, and it was to be taken for granted that I was, in the language of prudery, perfectly innocent. Leonora, to be consistent in goodness, or to complete her triumph in the face of the world, invited me to accompany her to the country.—I have now been some weeks at this superb castle. Heaven is my witness that I came with a heart overflowing with affection; but the painful, the agonizing sense of humiliation mixed with my tenderest sentiments, and all became bitterness insufferable. Oh, Gabrielle! you, and perhaps you alone upon earth, can understand my feelings. Adieu!—pity me—I must not ask you a single question about—I must not write the name for ever dear—What am I saying? where are my promises?—Adieu!—Adieu!

Your unhappy

OLIVIA.

LETTER XVI

MRS. C— TO MISS B—.

July 16th.

As I have never thought it my duty in this mortal life to mourn for the absurdities of my fellow-creatures, I should now enjoy the pleasure of laughing at Lady Olivia, if my propensity were not checked by a serious apprehension that she will injure Leonora's happiness. From the most generous motives, dear Leonora is continually anxious to soothe her mind, to persuade and reason her into common sense, to re-establish her in public opinion, and to make her happy. But I am convinced that Lady Olivia never will have common sense, and consequently never can be happy. Twenty times a day I wish her at the antipodes, for I dread lest Leonora should be implicated in her affairs, and involved in her misery.

Last night this foolish woman, who unluckily is graced with all the power of words, poured forth a fine declamation in favour of divorce. In vain Leonora reasoned, expostulated, blushed. Lady Olivia cannot blush for herself; and though both Mr. L— and I were present, she persisted with that vehemence which betrays personal interest in an argument. I suspect that she is going to try to obtain a divorce from her husband, that she may marry her lover. Consider the consequences of this for Leonora.—Leonora to be the friend of a woman who will risk the infamy of a trial at Doctors' Commons! But Leonora says I am mistaken, and that all this is only Olivia's way of talking. I wish then, that, if she does not intend to act like a fool, she would not talk like one. I agree with the gentleman who said that a woman who begins by playing the fool, always ends by playing the devil. Even before me, though I certainly never solicit her confidence, Lady Olivia talks with the most imprudent openness of her love affairs; not, I think, from ingenuousness, but from inability to restrain herself. Begin what subject of conversation I will, as far from Cupid as possible, she will bring me back again to him before I know where I am. She has no ideas but on this one subject. Leonora, dear, kind-hearted Leonora, attributes this to the temporary influence of a violent passion, which she assures me Olivia will conquer, and that then all her great and good qualities will, as if freed from enchantment, re-assume their natural vigour. Natural!—there is nothing natural about this sophisticated lady. I wish Leonora would think more of herself, and less of other people. As to Lady Olivia's excessive sensibility, I have no faith in it. I do not think either the lover or the passion so much to be feared for her, as the want of a lover and the habit of thinking that it is necessary to be in love. . . .

Yours affectionately,

HELEN C—.

GENERAL B— TO MR. L—.

MY DEAR L—, Paris, Hotel de Courlande,

When you ask a countryman in England the way to the next town, he replies, "Where do you come from, master?" and till you have answered this question, no information can you obtain from him. You ask me what I know of Lady Olivia —. What is your reason for asking? Till you have answered this question, hope for no information from me. Seriously, Lady Olivia had left Paris before I arrived, therefore you cannot have my judgment of her ladyship, which I presume is all you could depend upon. If you will take hearsay evidence, and if you wish me to speak to general character, I can readily satisfy you. Common reputed, loud and unanimous in favour of her talents, beauty, and fashion: there is no resisting, I am told, the fascination of her manners and conversation; but her opinions are fashionably liberal, and her practice as liberal as her theories. Since her separation from her husband, her lover is publicly named. Some English friends plead in her favour platonic attachment: this, like benefit of clergy, is claimed of course for a first offence: but Lady Olivia's Parisian acquaintance are not so scrupulous or so old-fashioned as to think it an offence; they call it an arrangement, and to this there can be no objection. As a French gentleman said to me the other day, with an unanswerable shrug, "Tout le monde sait que R— est son amant; d'ailleurs, c'est la femme la plus aimable du monde."

As to Lady Olivia's friend, Mad. de P—, she sees a great deal of company: her house is the resort of people of various descriptions; ministers, foreigners, coquettes, and generals; in short, of all those who wish, without scandal or suspicion, to intrigue either in love or politics. Her assemblies are also frequented by a few of l'ancien regime, who wish to be in favour with the present government. Mad. de P—, of a noble family herself, and formerly much at court, has managed matters so as to have regained all her husband's confiscated property, and to have acquired much influence with some of the leading men of the day. In her manners and conversation there is an odd mixture of frivolity and address, of the airs of coquetry and the jargon of sentiment. She has the politeness of a French Countess, with exquisite knowledge of the world and of les convenances, joined to that freedom of opinion which marks the present times. In the midst of all these inconsistencies, it is difficult to guess what her real character may be. At first sight I should pronounce her to be a silly woman, governed by vanity and the whim of the moment: but those who know her better than I do, believe her to be a woman of considerable talents, inordinately fond of power, and uniformly intent upon her own interest, using coquetry only as a means to govern our sex, and frivolity as a mask for her ambition. In short, Mad. de P— is a perfect specimen of the combination of an intrigante and an élégante, a combination often found in Paris. Here women mingle politics and gallantry—men mix politics and epicurism—which is the better mixture?

I have business of importance to my country to transact to-day, therefore I am going to dine with the modern Apicius. Excuse me, my dear friend, if I cannot stay at present to answer your questions about divorce. I must be punctual. What sort of a negotiator can he make who is too late at a minister's dinner? Five minutes might change the face of Europe.

Yours truly,

J. B.

LETTER XVIII

MADAME DE P— TO OLIVIA.

Paris.

My incomparable Olivia! your letters are absolutely divine. I am maussade, I vegetate. I cannot be said to live the days when I do not hear from you. Last Thursday I was disappointed of one of these dear letters, and Brave-et-tendre told me frankly, that I was so little amiable he should not have known me.— As to the rest, pardon me for not writing punctually: I have been really in a chaos of business and pleasure, and I do not know which fatigues most. But I am obliged to attend the ministers every day, for the sake of my friends.

A thousand and a thousand thanks for your pictures of your English friends: sketches by a masterly hand must be valuable, whatever the subject. I would rather have the pictures than the realities. Your Helen and your Lady Leonora are too good for me, and I pity you from my soul for being shut up in that old castle. I suppose it is like an old castle in Dauphiny, where I once spent a week, and where I was nearly frightened to death by the flapping of the old tapestry behind my bed, and by the bats which flew in through the broken windows. They say, however, that our chateaux and yours are something different. Of this I have no clear conception.

I send you three comforters in your prison—a billet-doux, a new novel, and a pattern of my sandal: a billet-doux from R— says every thing for itself; but I must say something for the new novel. Zenobie, which I now send you, is the declared rival of Seraphin. Parties have run high on both sides, and applications were made and inuendoes discovered, and wit and sentiment came to close combat; and, as usual, people talked till they did not understand themselves. For a fortnight, wherever one went, the first words to be heard on entering every salon were Seraphine and Zenobie.—Peace or war.—Mlle. Georges and Mlle. Duchesnois were nothing to Seraphine and Zenobie. For Heaven's sake tell me which you prefer! But I fear they will be no more talked of before I have your answer. To say the truth, I am tired of both heroines, for a fortnight is too long to talk or think of any one thing.

I flatter myself you will like my sandals: they are my own invention, and my foot really shows them to advantage. You know I might say, as Du P— said of himself, "J'ai un pied dont la petitesse échappe à la vitesse de la pensée." I thought my poor friend Mad. Dumarais would have died with envy, the other day, when I appeared in them at her ball, which, by-the-bye, was in all its decorations as absurd and in as bad taste as usual. For the most part these nouveaux riches lavish money, but can never purchase taste or a sense of propriety. All is gold: but that is not enough; or rather that is too much. In spite of all that both the Indies, China, Arabia, Egypt, and even Paris can do for them, they will be ever out of place, in the midst of their magnificence: they will never even know how to ruin themselves nobly. They must live and die as they were born, ridiculous. Now I would rather not exist than feel myself ridiculous. But I believe no one living, not even le petit d'Heronville, knows himself to be an object of ridicule. There are no looking-glasses for the mind, and I question whether we should use them if there were. D'Heronville is just as you left him, and as much my amusement as he used to be yours. He goes on with an eternal galimatias of patriotism, with such a self-sufficient air and decided tone! never suspecting that he says only what other people make him say, and that he is listened to, only to find out what some people think. Many will say before fools, what they would not hazard before wise men; not considering that fools can repeat as well as parrots. I once heard a great man remark, that the only spies fit to be trusted are those who do not know themselves to be such; who have no salary but what their vanity pays them, and who are employed without being accredited.

But trove de politique!—My charming Olivia, I know, abhors politics, as much as I detest metaphysics, from all lips or pens but hers. Now I must tell you something of your friends here.

O— talks nonsense as agreeably as ever, and dances as divinely. 'Tis a pity he cannot always dance, for then he would not ruin himself at play. He wants me to get him a regiment—as if I had any power!—or as if I would use it for this purpose, when I knew that my interesting friend Mad. Q— would break her poor little heart if he were to quit her.

Mon Coeur is as pretty as ever; but she is now in affliction. She has lost her dear little dog Corisonde. He died suddenly; almost in her arms! She will erect a monument to him in her charming jardin Anglois. This will occupy her, and then "Time, the comforter"—Inimitable Voltaire!

Our dear Brillante has just had a superb hommage from her lover the commissary—a necklace and bracelets of the finest; pearls: but she cannot wear them yet: her brother having died last week, she is in deep mourning. This brother was not upon good terms with her. He never forgave the divorce. He thought it a disgrace to have a sister une divorcee; but he was full of prejudice, poor man, and he is dead, and we need think no more of him or of his faults.

Our ci-devant chanoine, who married that little Meudon, is as miserable as possible, and as ridiculous: for he is jealous of his young wife, and she is a franche-coquette. The poor man looks as if he repented sincerely of his errors. What a penitent a coquette can make of a husband! Bourdaloue and Massillon would have tried their powers on this man's heart in vain.

Did I tell you that Mad. G— is a second time divorced? But this time it is her husband's doing, not hers. This handsome husband has spent all the immense fortune she brought him, and now procures a divorce for incompatibility of temper, and is going to marry another lady, richer than Mad. G—, and as great a fool. This system of divorce, though convenient, is not always advantageous to women. However, in one point of view, I wonder that the rigid moralists do not defend it, as the only means of making a man in love with his own wife. A man divorces; the law does not permit him to marry the same woman afterwards; of course this prohibition makes him fall in love with her. Of this we have many edifying examples besides Fanchette, who, though she was so beautiful, and a tolerable actress, would never have drawn all Paris to the Vaudeville if she had not been a divorcee, and if it had not been known that her husband, who played the lover of the piece, was dying to marry her again. Apropos, Mad. St. Germain is acting one of her own romances, in the high sublime style, and threatens to poison herself for love of her perjured inconstant—but it will not do.

Madame la Grande was near having a sad accident the other night: in crossing the Pont-neuf her horses took fright; for there was a crowd and embarras, a man having just drowned himself—not for love, but for hunger. How many men, women, and children, do you think drowned themselves in the Seine last year? Upwards of two hundred. This is really shocking, and a stop should be put to it by authority. It absolutely makes me shudder and reflect; but apres nous le deluge was La Pompadour's maxim, and should be ours.

Mad. Folard se coiffe en cheveux, and Mad. Rocroix crowns herself with roses, whilst all the world knows that either of them is old enough to be my mother. In former days a woman could not wear flowers after thirty, and was bel esprit or devote at forty, for it was thought bad taste to do otherwise. But now every body may be as young as they please, or as ridiculous. Women have certainly gained by the new order of things.

Our poor friend Vermeille se meurt de la poitrine—a victim to tea and late hours. She is an interesting creature, and my heart bleeds for her: she will never last till winter.

Do you know, it is said, we shall soon have no wood to burn. What can have become of all our forests? People should inquire after them. The Venus de Medici has at last found her way down the Seine. It is not determined yet where to place her: but she is at Paris, and that is a great point gained for her. You complained that the Apollo stands with his back so near the wall, that there is no seeing half the beauties of his shoulders. If I have any influence, Venus shall not be so served. I have been to see her. She is certainly divine—but not French. I do not despair of seeing her surpassed by our artists.

Adieu, my adorable Olivia. I should have finished my letter yesterday; but when I came home in the morning, expecting to have a moment sacred to you and friendship, whom should I find established in an arm-chair in my cabinet but our old Countess Cidevant. There was no retreat for me. In the midst of my concentrated rage, I was obliged to advance and embrace her, and there was an end of happiness for the day. The pitiless woman kept me till it was even too late to dress, talking over her family misfortunes; as if they were any thing to me. She wants to get her son employed, but her pride will not let her pay her court properly, and she wants me to do it for her. Not I, truly. I should shut my doors against her but for the sake of her nephew le roue, who is really a pretty young man. My angel, I embrace you tenderly.

GABRIELLE DE P—.

LETTER XIX

OLIVIA TO MADAME DE P—.

How melancholy to a feeling heart is the moment when illusion vanishes, whether that illusion has been created by the magic of love or of friendship! How many such moments, Gabrielle, has your unfortunate friend been doomed to endure! Alas! when will treacherous fancy cease to throw a deceitful brilliancy upon each new object!

Perhaps I am too delicate—but R—'s note, enclosed in your last, my Gabrielle, was unlike his former letters. It was not passionate, it was only reasonable. A man who can reason is no longer in love. The manner in which he speaks of divorce shocked me beyond expression. Is it for him to talk of scruples when upon this subject I have none? I own to you that my pride and my tenderness are sensibly wounded. Is it for him to convince me that I am in the wrong? I shall not be at ease till I hear from you again, my amiable friend: for my residence here becomes insupportable. But a few short weeks are past since I fancied Leonora an angel, and now she falls below the ordinary standard of mortals. But a few short weeks are past since, in the full confidence of finding in Leonora a second self, a second Gabrielle, I eagerly developed to her my inmost soul; yet now my heart closes, I fear never more to open. The sad conviction, that we have but few ideas, and no feelings in common, stops my tongue when I attempt to speak, chills my heart when I begin to listen.

Do you know, my Gabrielle, I have discovered that Leonora is inordinately selfish? For all other faults I have charity; but selfishness, which has none to give, must expect none. O divine sensibility, defend me from this isolation of the heart! All thy nameless sorrows, all thy heart-rending tortures, would I a thousand times rather endure. Leonora's selfishness breaks out perpetually; and, alas! it is of the most inveterate, incurable kind: every thing that is immediately or remotely connected with self she loves, and loves with the most provoking pertinacity. Her mother, her husband, she adores, because they are her own; and even her sister's children, because she considers them, she says, as her own. All and every possible portion of self she cherishes with the most sordid partiality. All that touches these relations touches her; and every thing which is theirs, or, in other words, which is hers, she deems excellent and sacred. Last night I just hazarded a word of ridicule upon some of the obsolete prejudices of that august personage, that Duchess of old tapestry, her still living ancestor. I wish, Gabrielle, you had seen Leonora's countenance. Her colour rose up to her temples, her eyes lightened with indignation, and her whole person assumed a dignity, which might have killed a presumptuous lover, or better far, might have enslaved him for life. What folly to waste all this upon such an occasion! But selfishness is ever blind to its real interests. Leonora is so bigoted to this old woman, that she is already in mind an old woman herself. She fancies that she traces a resemblance to her mother, and of course to dear self in her infant, and she looks upon it with such doting eyes, and talks to it with such exquisite tones of fondness, as are to me, who know the source from which they proceed, quite ridiculous and disgusting. An infant, who has no imaginable merit, and, to impartial eyes, no charms, she can love to this excess from no motive but pure egotism. Then her husband—but this subject I must reserve for another letter. I am summoned to walk with him this moment.

Adieu, charming Gabrielle,

OLIVIA.

LETTER XX

GENERAL B— TO MR. L—.

MY DEAR L—, Paris, 180—.

Enclosed I send you, according to your earnest desire, Cambaceres' reflections upon the intended new law of divorce. Give me leave to ask why you are so violently interested upon this occasion? Do you envy France this blessing? Do you wish that English husbands and wives should have the power of divorcing each other at pleasure for incompatibility of temper? And have you calculated the admirable effect this would produce upon the temper both of the weaker and the stronger sex? To bear and forbear would then be no longer necessary. Every happy pair might quarrel and part at a moment's notice—at a year's notice at most. And their children? The wisdom of Solomon would be necessary to settle the just division of the children. I have this morning been attending a court of law to hear a famous trial between two husbands: the abdicated lord a ci-devant noble, and the reigning husband a ci-devant grand-vicaire, who has reformed. Each party claimed a right to the children by the first marriage, for the children were minors entitled to large fortunes. The reformed grand-vicaire pleaded his own cause with astonishing assurance, amidst the discountenancing looks, murmurs, and almost amidst the groans of disapprobation from the majority of the auditors. His powers of impudence, however, failed him at last. I sat on the bench behind him, and saw that his ears had the grace to blush. After another hearing, this cause, which had lasted four years, was decided; and the first husband and real father was permitted to have the guardianship of his own children. During the four years' litigation, the friends of the parties, from the grandmother downwards, were all at irreconcileable variance. What became of the children all this time? Their mother was represented during the trial as she deserved to be, as a wretch void of shame and gratitude. The father was universally pitied, though his rival painted him as a coward, who during the revolution had left his children to save himself by flight; and as a fool, who had left his wife to the care of a profligate grand-vicaire. Divorce is not countenanced by opinion in Paris, though permitted by law. With a few exceptions in extraordinary cases, I have observed that les divorcees are not received into good society.

To satiate your curiosity, I send you all the papers that have been written lately on this subject, of which you will find that of Cambacérès the best. The wits say that he is an impartial judge. I presume you want these pamphlets for some foolish friend; for yourself you can never want them, blessed as you are with such a wife as Lady Leonora L—. I am not surprised that profligate men should wish for freedom of divorce, because it would save them damages in Doctors' Commons: but you rather astonish me—if a wise man should be astonished at any thing in these days—by assuring me that you have lately heard this system eloquently defended by a female philosopher. What can women expect from it but contempt? Next to polygamy, it would prove the most certain method of destroying the domestic happiness of the sex, as well as their influence and respectability in society. But some of the dear creatures love to talk of what they do not understand, and usually show their eloquence to the greatest advantage, by taking the wrong side of a question.

Yours truly,

J. B.

OLIVIA TO MADAME DE P—.

L— Castle.

From selfishness to jealousy there is but one step, or rather there is none; for jealousy of a certain sort is but selfishness in another form. How different this passion as I have felt it, and as I see it shown! In some characters it is the symptom of amiable and exquisite sensibility; in others of odious coldness and contraction of heart. In some of our sex it is, you know, my Gabrielle, a delicate fear, a tender anxiety, a proof of ardent passion; in others it is a mere love of power, a disgusting struggle for the property of a heart, an absurd assertion of rights and prerogatives. Surely no prejudice of education or institution can be more barbarous than that which teaches a wife that she has an indefeasible and exclusive right both to the affections and the fidelity of her husband. I am astonished to hear it avowed by any woman who has the slightest pretensions to delicacy of sentiment, or liberality of mind. I should expect to find this vulgar prejudice only among the downright dames, who talk of my good man, and lay a particular emphasis on the possessive pronoun my; who understand literally, and expect that their spouses should adhere punctually to every coarse article of our strange marriage vow.

In certain points of view, my Gabrielle, jealousy is undoubtedly the strongest proof of an indelicate mind. Yet, if I mistake not, the delicate, the divine Leonora, is liable to this terrestrial passion. Yesterday evening, as I was returning from a stroll in the park with Mr. L—, we met Leonora; and methought she looked embarrassed at meeting us. Heaven knows there was not the slightest occasion for embarrassment, and I could not avoid being surprised at such weakness, I had almost said folly, in a woman of Leonora's sense, especially as she knows how my heart is attached. In the first moments of our intimacy my confidence was unbounded, as it ever is in those I love. Aware as I was of the light in which the prejudices of her education and her country make her view such connexions, yet I scrupled not, with the utmost candour, to confess the unfortunate attachment which had ruled my destiny. After this confidence, do not suspicion and jealousy on her part appear strange? Were Mr. L— and I shut up for life in the same prison, were we left together upon a desert island, were we alone in the universe, I could never think of him. And Leonora does not see this! How the passions obscure and degrade the finest understandings! But perhaps I do her injustice, and she felt nothing of what her countenance expressed. It is certain, however, that she was silent for some moments after she joined us, from what cause she knows best—so was Mr. L—, I suppose from English awkwardness—so was I, from pure astonishment. At length, in pity of Leonora, I broke the silence. I had recourse to the beauties of nature.

"What a heavenly evening!" said I. "We have been listening to the songs of the birds, enjoying this fresh breeze of nature's perfumes." Leonora said something about the superiority of nature's perfumes to those of art; and observed, "how much more agreeable the smell of flowers appears in the open air than in confined rooms!" Whilst she spoke she looked at her husband, as she continually does for assent and approbation. He assented, but apparently without knowing what he was saying; and only by one of his English monosyllables. I alone was at ease.

"Can any thing be more beautiful," continued I, looking back, "than the soft mellow foliage of those woods, and the exquisite tints of their rich colouring? What delicious melancholy such an evening spreads over the heart!—what reflections!—what recollections!—Oh, Leonora, look at the lights upon that mountain, and the deep shadows upon the lake below. Just such scenes have I admired, by such have I been entranced in Switzerland."

Leonora put her arm within mine—she seemed to have no objection to my thoughts going back to Switzerland—I sighed—she pressed my hand affectionately—I wiped the starting tear from my eye. Mr. L— looked at me with something like surprise whilst I repeated involuntarily,

"I mourn, but, ye woodlands, I mourn not for you,
For morn is approaching your charms to restore,
Perfumed with fresh fragrance, and glitt'ring with dew."

I paused, recollecting myself, struck with the ridicule of repeating verses, and of indulging feelings in which no one perhaps sympathized.

"Those are beautiful lines," said Leonora: "that poem has always been a favourite of mine."

"And of mine, also," said Mr. L—.

"I prefer Beattie's Hermit to all other hermits," said Leonora.

I was not in a mood calmly to discuss with her a point of criticism—I walked on in reverie: but in this I was not allowed to indulge. Mr. L— asked if I could not recollect some more of the Hermit—I pleaded the worst memory in the world—a memory that can never recollect any poem perfectly by rote, only the touches of genius or sensibility that strike me—and those are so few!

"But in this poem there are so many," said Leonora. I am sure she insisted only to please her husband, and pleaded against her real feelings, purposely to conceal them. He persisted in his request, with more warmth than usual. I was compelled to rouse myself from my reverie, and to call back my distant thoughts. I repeated all that I could recollect of the poem. Mr. L— paid me a profusion of compliments upon the sweetness of my voice, and my taste in reciting. He was pleased to find that my manner and tones gave an Italian expression to English poetry, which to him was a peculiar charm. It reminded him of some Signora, whom he had known at Florence. This was the first time I had learned that he had been abroad. I was going to explore the foreign field of conversation which he thus opened; but just at that moment Leonora withdrew her arm from mine, and I fancied that she coloured. This might be only my fancy, or the natural effect of her stooping to gather a flower. We were now within sight of the castle. I pointed to one of the turrets over a Gothic window, upon which the gleams of the setting sun produced a picturesque effect; my glove happened to be off, and Leonora unluckily saw that her husband's eyes were fixed upon my arm, instead of the turret to which I was pointing. 'Twas a trifle which I never should have noticed, had she not forced it upon my attention. She actually turned pale. I had the presence of mind not to put on my glove.

I must observe more accurately; I must decide whether this angelic Leonora is, or is not susceptible of the mortal passion ycleped jealousy. I confess my curiosity is awakened.

Adieu, my ever amiable Gabrielle. OLIVIA.

LETTER XXII

OLIVIA TO MADAME DE P—.

When the passions are asleep we are apt to fancy they are dead. I verily thought that curiosity was dead within me, it had lain so long dormant, while stronger and tenderer sentiments waked in full activity; but now that absence and distance from their object lull them to temporary repose, the vulgar subordinate passions are roused, and take their turn to reign. My curiosity was so strongly excited upon the subject of Leonora's jealousy, that I could not rest, without attempting to obtain satisfaction. Blame me not, dearest Gabrielle, for in my situation you would inevitably have done the same, only that you would have done it with more address; with that peculiar, inimitable address, which I envy above all your accomplishments. But address is a delicate native of France, and though it may now and then exist as a stranger, I doubt whether it can ever be naturalized in our rude climate. All the attempts I have made are, however, encouraging enough—you shall judge. My object was, to ascertain the existence or non-existence of Leonora's jealousy. I set about it with a tolerably careless assurance, and followed up the hint which accident had thrown out for my ingenuity to work upon. You remember, or at least I remember, that Leonora withdrew her arm from mine, and stooped to gather a flower at the moment when her husband mentioned Florence, and the resemblance of my voice to that of some Italian charmer. The next day I happened to play some of my sweetest Italian airs, and to accompany them with my voice. The music-room opens into the great hall: Leonora and her husband were in the hall, talking to some visitors. The voices were soon hushed, as I expected, by the magic sounds, but, what I did not expect, Leonora was the first who led the way into the music-room. Was this affectation? These simple characters sometimes baffle all the art of the decipherer. I should have been clear that it was affectation, had Leonora been prodigal of compliments on my performance; but she seemed only to listen for her own pleasure, and left it to Mr. L— to applaud. Whilst I was preparing to play over again the air which pleased him most, the two little nephews came running to beg Leonora would follow them to look at some trifle, some coloured shadow, upon the garden-wall, I think they said: she let them lead her off, leaving us together. This did not seem like jealousy. I was more at a loss than ever, and determined to make fresh and more decisive experiments. Curiosity, you know, is heightened by doubt. To cure myself of curiosity, it is necessary therefore to put my mind out of doubt. Admire the practical application of metaphysics! But metaphysics always make you yawn. Adieu for to-day.

OLIVIA.

MRS. C— TO MISS B—.

L— Castle.

Dear Margaret, an uncle of mine, who, ever since I can remember, seemed to me cut out for an old bachelor, writes me word that he is just going to be married, and that I must grace his nuptials. I cannot refuse, for he has always been very kind to me, and we have no right to cut people out for old bachelors. That I am sorry to leave Leonora, it is superfluous to tell you; but this is the melancholy part of the business, on which I make it a principle to dwell as little as possible.

Lady Olivia must be heartily glad that I am going, for I have been terribly troublesome to her by my gaiety and my simplicity. I shall lose all the pleasure I had promised myself in seeing the denouement of the comedy of The Sentimental Coquette; or, The Heroine unmasked.

I made Leonora almost angry with me this morning, by a hint or two I gave upon this subject. She looked so very grave, that I was afraid of my own thoughts, and I dared not explain myself farther. Intimate as I am with her, there are points on which I am sure that she would never make me her confidante. I think that she has not been in her usual good spirits lately; and though she treats Olivia with uniform kindness, and betrays not, even to my watchful eyes, the slightest symptom of jealousy, yet I suspect that she sees what is going forward, and she suffers in secret. Now, if she would let me explain myself, I could set her heart at ease, by the assurance that Mr. L— is only acting a part. If her affection for her husband did not almost blind her, she would have as much penetration as I have—which you will allow, my dear Margaret, is saying a great deal.

Yours affectionately,

HELEN C—.

OLIVIA TO MADAME DE P—.

L— Castle.

Congratulate me, my charming Gabrielle, upon being delivered from the unfeeling gaiety of that friend of Leonora, that Helen of whom I formerly sent you a too flattering portrait. Her departure relieves me from many painful sensations. Dissonance to a musical ear is not more horrid, than want of harmony between characters, to the soul of sensibility. Between Helen and me there was a perpetual discord of ideas and sentiments, which fatigued me inexpressibly. Besides, I began to consider her as a spy upon my actions. But there, I believe, I did her injustice, for she was too much occupied with her own trifling thoughts to have any alarming powers of observation.

Since her departure we have been very gay. Yesterday we had a large company at dinner; some of the neighbouring families, whom I expected to find mere country visitors, that were come a dozen miles to show their antediluvian finery, retire half an hour after dinner, spoil coffee with cream, say nothing, but at their appointed hours rise, ring for their superb carriages, and go home by moonlight. However, to my astonishment, I found myself in a society of well-bred, well-informed persons; the women ready to converse, and the men, even after dinner, not impatient to get rid of them. Two or three of the company had travelled, and I was glad to talk to them of Italy, Switzerland, and France. Mr. L— I knew would join in this conversation. I discovered that he came to Florence just as I was leaving it. I was to have been at our ambassador's one evening when he was there; but a headache prevented me. These little coincidences, you know, my Gabrielle, draw people closer together. I remember to have heard of a Mr. L— at Florence, who was a passionate admirer of our sex. He was then unmarried. I little thought that this was the same person. Beneath a cold exterior these Englishmen often conceal a wondrous quantity of enthusiasm—volcanoes under snow. Curiosity, dear indefatigable curiosity, supported me through the labour of clearing away the snow, and I came to indubitable traces of unextinguished and unextinguishable fire. The character of L— is quite different from what I had imagined it to be. It is an excellent study. We had a long and interesting conversation upon national manners, especially upon those of the females of all nations. He concluded by quoting the words of your friend M. le Vicomte de

Segur, "If I were permitted to choose, I should prefer a French woman for my friend, an English woman for my wife, and a Polish lady for my mistress."

From this, it seems, that I am mistaken about the Italian signora, or else Mr. L— has an enlarged charity for the graces of all nations.—More subject for curiosity.

In the evening, before the company separated, we were standing on the steps of the great hall, looking at a fine effect of moonlight, and I pointed out the shadow of the arches of a bridge. From moonlight we went on to lamplight, and many pretty things were said about art and nature. A gentleman, who had just returned from Paris, talked of the reflection of the lamps in the Seine, which one sees in crossing the Pont-Royal, and which, as he said, appear like a colonnade of fire. As soon as he had finished prosing about his colonnade, I turned to Mr. L—, and asked if he remembered the account which Coxe the traveller gives of the Polish princess Czartoryski's charming fête champêtre and the illuminated rustic bridge of one arch, the reflection of which in the water was so strong as to deceive the eye, and to give the whole the appearance of a brilliant circle suspended in the air. Mr. L— seemed enchanted with my description, and eagerly said that he would some night have a bridge in his improvements, illuminated, that we (half-gallant Englishman!) might see the effect. I carelessly replied, that probably it would have a good effect: I would then have talked on other subjects to the lady next me: but an Englishman cannot suddenly change the course of his conversation. Mr. L— still persisted in asking a variety of questions about this Polish fête. I excused myself; for if you satisfy curiosity you are no longer sublime; besides it is so pedantic to remember accurately any thing one meets with in books. I assured him that I had forgotten the particulars.

My countrymen are wondrous persevering, when once roused. This morning, when I came down to breakfast, I found Mr. L— with a volume of Coxe's travels in his hand. He read aloud to Leonora the whole description of the illuminated gardens, and of a Turkish tent of curious workmanship, and of a pavilion, supported by pillars, ornamented with wreaths of flowers. Leonora's birthday is some time in the next month; and her husband, probably to prevent any disagreeable little feelings, proposed that the fête champêtre, he designed to give, should be on that day. She seemed rather to discourage the thing. Now to what should this indifference be attributed? To jealousy I should positively decide, but that two reasons oppose this idea, and keep me in doubt. She was not within hearing at the moonlight conference, and knew nothing of my having mentioned the Polish fête, or of her husband's having proposed to illuminate the bridge for me. Besides, I remember, the other day when she was reading the new French novel you sent me, she expressed great dislike to the sentimental fêtes, which the lover prepares for his mistress. I would give more than I dare tell you, my dear Gabrielle, to be able to decide whether she is jealous of me or not. But where was I? Mr. L—, who had set his heart upon the fête champêtre, persisted, and combatted her antipathy by reason. Foolish man! he should have tried compliments, or caresses—if I had not been present.

"My dear Leonora," said he, "I think you carry your dislike to these things too far. They are more according to the French than to the English taste, I know; but we should not be influenced by national prejudice. I detest the ostentation and the affectation of sentiment as much as you can; but where the real feeling exists, every mode of showing kindness is agreeable. You must let us have this little fête on your birthday. Besides the pleasure it will give me, I really think it is useful to mix ideas of affection with amusement."

She smiled most graciously, and replied, that she would with pleasure accept of kindness in any form from him. In short, she was willing to have the fête, when it was clearly explained that she was to be the object of it. Is not this proof positive of jealousy? And yet my curiosity is not thoroughly satisfied. I must go on; for Leonora's sake I must go on. When I have been assured of the truth, I shall know how to conduct myself; and you, who know my heart, will do me the justice to believe, that when I am convinced of my friend's weakness, I shall spare it with the most delicate caution: but till I am convinced, I am in perpetual danger of blundering by my careless, inadvertent innocence. You smile, Gabrielle; dear malicious Gabrielle, even in your malice you are charming! Adieu! Pray for the speedy extinction of my curiosity.

OLIVIA.

LETTER XXV

LEONORA TO HER MOTHER.

You say, my dearest mother, that of late, my letters have been more constrained and less cheerful than usual, and you conjure me not to conceal from you any thing which may concern my happiness. I have ever found you my best and most indulgent friend, and there is not a thought or feeling of my mind, however weak or foolish, that I desire to conceal from you. No one in this world is more—is so much interested in my happiness; and, in every doubtful situation, I have always been accustomed to apply to your unerring judgment for assistance. Your strength of mind, your enlightened affection, would support and direct me, would at once show me how I ought to act, and inspire me with courage and fortitude sufficient to be worthy of your esteem and of my own. At no period of my life, not even when my heart first felt the confused sensations of a passion that was new to it, did I ever want or wish for a friend so much as at this instant: and yet I hesitate whether I ought to ask even your advice, whether I ought to indulge myself in speaking of my feelings even to my mother. I refrained from giving the slightest intimation of them to my dear Helen, though she often led to this subject, and seemed vexed by my reserve. I thought it not right to accept of her sympathy. From her kindness I had every consolation to expect, but no assistance from her counsels, because she does not understand Mr. L—'s character, and I could plainly perceive that she had an erroneous idea so fixed in her fancy, as to prevent her seeing things in their true light. I am afraid of imputing blame where I most wish to avoid it: I fear to excite unjust suspicions; I dread that if I say the whole, you will imagine that I mean much more than I say.

I have not been quite well lately, and my mind probably is more apt to be alarmed than it would be, if my health were stronger. All that I apprehend, may exist merely in my own distempered imagination. Do not then suppose others are to blame, when perhaps I only am in fault. I have for some time past been dissatisfied with myself, and have had reason to be so: I do not say this from any false humility; I despise that affectation; but I say it with a sincere desire that you may assist me to cure myself of a weakness, which, if it were to grow upon my mind, must render me miserable, and might destroy the happiness of the person I love best upon earth. You know that I am not naturally or habitually of a suspicious temper, but I am conscious of having lately felt a disposition to jealousy. I have been spoiled by the excessive attention, which my husband paid to me in the first year of our marriage.

You warned me not to fancy that he could continue always a lover. I did not, at least I tried not to expect such an impossibility. I was prepared for the change, at least I thought I was: yet now the time, the inevitable time is come, and I have not the fortitude to bear it as I ought. If I had never known what it was to possess his love, I might perhaps be content with his friendship. If I could feel only friendship for him, I should now, possibly, be happy. I know that I have the first place in his esteem: I do believe—I should be miserable indeed if I did not believe—that I have the first place in his affection. But this affection is certainly different from what it once was. I wish I could forget the difference. No: I retract that wish; however painful the comparison, the recollection of times that are past is delightful to my heart. Yet, my dear mother, if such times are never to return, it would be better for me to forget that they have ever been. It would be wiser not to let my imagination recur to the past, which could then tend only to render me discontented with the present and with the future. The FUTURE! how melancholy that word sounds to me! What a dreary length of prospect it brings to my view! How young I am, how many years may I have to live, and how little motive have I left in life! Those which used to act most forcibly upon me, have now scarcely power to move my mind. The sense of duty, it is true, raises me to some degree of exertion; I hope that I do not neglect the education of the two children whom my poor sister bequeathed to my care. When my mind was at ease they were my delight; but now I feel that I am rather interrupted than interested by their childish gaiety and amusements.

I am afraid that I am growing selfish, and I am sure that I have become shamefully indolent. I go on with certain occupations every day from habit, not from choice; my mind is not in them. I used to flatter myself that I did many things, from a sense of duty and of general benevolence, which I am convinced were done merely from a particular wish to please, and to make myself more and more beloved by the object of my fondest affection. Disappointed in this hope, I sink into indolence, from which the desire to entertain my friends is not sufficient to rouse me. Helen has been summoned away; but I believe I told you that Mr. and Mrs. F—, whose company is peculiarly agreeable to my taste, and Lady M— and her amiable daughters, and your witty friend —, are with us. In such society I am ashamed of being stupid; yet I cannot contribute to the amusement of the company, and I feel surprised at their animation and sprightliness. It seems as if I was looking on at dances, without hearing any music. Sometimes I fear that my silence should be observed, and then I begin to talk, without well knowing what I am saying. I confine myself to the most common-place subjects, and hesitate, from the dread of saying something quite foreign to the purpose. What must Mr. L— think of my stupidity? But he does not, I believe, perceive it: he is so much occupied with—with other objects. I am glad that he does not see all that passes in my mind, for he might despise me if he knew that I am so miserable. I did not mean to use so strong an expression; but now it is written, I will not blot it out, lest you should fancy something worse than the reality. I am not, however, yet so weak as to be seriously miserable when I have no real cause to be so. The truth is —. Now you know this phrase is a tacit confession that all that has been said before is false. The real truth is —. By my prefacing so long you may he sure that I have reason to be ashamed of this real truth's coming out. The real truth is, that I have been so long accustomed to be the first and only object of Mr. L—'s thoughts, that I cannot bear to see him think of any thing else. Yes, things I can bear; but not persons—female persons; and there is one person here, who is so much more agreeable and entertaining than I am, that she engrosses very naturally almost all his attention. I am not envious, I am sure; for I could once admire all Lady Olivia's talents and accomplishments, and no one could be more charmed than I was, with her fascinating manners and irresistible powers of pleasing; but when those irresistible powers may rob me of the heart of my beloved husband—of the whole happiness of my life—how can I admire them? All I can promise is to preserve my mind from the meanness of suspicion. I can do my rival justice. I can believe, and entreat you to believe, that she does not wish to be my rival: that she is perfectly innocent of all design to injure me, and that she is not aware of the impression she has made. I, who know every change of Mr. L—'s countenance, every inflexion of his voice, every turn of his mind, can see too plainly what she cannot discern. I should indeed have thought, that no woman, whom he distinguished or preferred in any degree, could avoid perceiving it, his manner is so expressive, so flattering; but perhaps this appears so only to me—a woman, who does not love him, may see things very differently. Lady Olivia can be in no danger, because her heart, fortunately for me, is prepossessed in favour of another; and a woman whose heart is occupied by one object is absolutely blind, as I well know, to all others. With this security I ought to be satisfied; for I believe no one inspires a lasting passion, without sharing it.

I am summoned to give my opinion about certain illuminations and decorations for a fête champêtre which Mr. L— is so kind as to give in honour of my birthday—just at the time I am complaining of his neglect!—No, dear mother, I hope I have not complained of him, but of myself:—and it is your business to teach your daughter to be more reasonable. Write soon and fully to

Your affectionate

LEONORA.

LETTER XXVI

OLIVIA TO MADAME DE P—.

This fine fête champêtre is over.—Expect no description of it from me, Gabrielle, for I am horribly out of humour. The whole pleasure of the evening was destroyed by the most foolish circumstance imaginable. Leonora's jealousy is now evident to more eyes than mine. No farther doubt upon the subject can remain. My curiosity is satisfied; but I am now left to reproach myself, for having gone so far to ascertain what I ought to have taken for granted. All these good English wives are jealous; so jealous, that no one, who has any pretensions to beauty, wit, or amiability, can live with them. They can have no society in our sense of the word; of course they must live shut up in their own dismal houses, with their own stupid families, the faithful husband and wife sitting opposite to each other in their own chimney corners, yawning models of constancy. And this they call virtue! How the meanest vices usurp the name of virtue! Leonora's is a jealousy of the most illiberal and degrading species; a jealousy of the temper, not of the heart. She is too cold to feel the passion of love.—She never could be in love; of that I am certain. She is too reasonable, too prudish. Besides, to imagine that she could be in love with her own husband, and after eighteen months' marriage—the thing is absurd! the thing is impossible! No, she deceives herself or him, or both, if she pretends that her jealousy arises from love, from what you and I, Gabrielle, understand by the word. Passion, and passion only, can plead a just excuse of its own excesses. Were Leonora in love, I could pardon her jealousy. But now I despise it. Yes, with all her high reputation, and imposing qualities, I must think of her with contempt. And now that I have given vent to my feelings, with that freedom in which I ever indulge myself in writing to you, my amiable Gabrielle, chosen friend of my heart, I will compose myself, and give you a rational account of things.

You know that I am said to have some taste. Leonora makes no pretensions to any. Wishing, I suppose, that her fête should be as elegant as possible, she consulted me about all the arrangements and decorations. It was I that did every thing. My skill and taste were admired by the whole company, and especially by Mr. L—. He was in remarkably good spirits at the commencement of the evening; quite gay and gallant: he certainly paid me a great deal of attention, and it was natural he should; for besides being his guest, I was undoubtedly the most elegant woman present. My fame had gone abroad; I found that I was the object of general attention. To this I have been tolerably well accustomed all my life; enough at least to prevent me from giving any visible sign of being moved by admiration in whatever form it comes; whether in the polite foreign glance, or the broad English stare. The starers enjoyed their pleasure, and I mine: I moved and talked, I smiled or was pensive, as though I saw them not; nevertheless the homage of their gaze was not lost upon me. You know, my charming Gabrielle, one likes to observe the sensation one produces amongst new people. The incense that I perceived in the surrounding atmosphere was just powerful enough to affect my nerves agreeably: that languor which you have so often reproached me for indulging in the company of what we call indifferents gradually dissipated; and, as poor R— used to say of me, I came from behind my cloud like the sun in all its glory. I was such as you have seen me, Gabrielle, in my best days, in my best moments, in my very best style. I wonder what would excite me to such a waste of powers. L— seemed inspired too: he really was quite agreeable, and showed me off almost as well as R— himself could have done. I had no idea that he had this species of talent. You will never know of what my countrymen are capable, for you are out of patience with the statues the first half hour: now it takes an amazing time to animate them; but they can be waked into life, and I have a pride in conquering difficulties.—There were more men this night, in proportion to the women, than one usually sees in English company, consequently it was more agreeable. I was surrounded by an admiring audience, and my conversation of course was sufficiently general to please all, and sufficiently particular to distinguish the man whom I wished to animate. In all this you will say there was nothing to put one out of humour, nothing very mortifying:—but stay, my fair philosopher, do not judge of the day till you see its end.—Leonora was so hid from my view by the crowd of adorers, that I really did not discern her, or suspect her jealousy. I was quite natural; I thought only of myself; I declined all invitations to dance, declaring that it was so long since I had tried an English country dance, that I dared not expose my awkwardness. French country dances were mentioned, but I preferred conversation. At last L— persecuted me to try a Polish dance with him—a multitude of voices overpowered me. I have not the talent which some of my countrywomen possess in such perfection, of being obstinate about trifles. When I can refuse with grace, 'tis well; but when that is no longer possible, it is my principle, or my weakness, to yield. I was surprised to find that L— danced admirably. I became animated. You know how dancing animates me, when I have a partner who can dance—a thing not very common in this country. We ended by waltzing, first in the Polish, and afterwards in the Parisian manner. I certainly surpassed myself—I flew, I was borne upon the wings of the wind, I floated on the notes of the music. Animated or languid in every gradation of grace and sentiment, I abandoned myself to the inspiration of the moment; I was all soul, and the spectators were all admiration. To you, my Gabrielle, I may speak thus of myself without vanity: you know the sensation I was accustomed to produce at Paris; you may guess then what the effect must be here, where such a style of dancing has all the captivation of novelty. Had I doubted that my success was complete, I should have been assured of it by the faces of some prudes amongst the matrons, who affected to think that the waltz was too much. As L— was leading, or rather supporting me to my seat, for I was quite exhausted, I overheard a gentleman, who was at no great distance from the place where Leonora was standing, whisper to his neighbour, "Le Valse extreme est la volupte permise." I fancy Leonora overheard these words, as well as myself, for my eyes met hers at this instant, and she coloured, and directly looked another way. L— neither heard nor saw any thing of all this: he was intent upon procuring me a seat; and an Englishman can never see or think of two things at a time. A few minutes afterwards, whilst he was fanning me, a young awkward peasant girl, quite a stranger in this country, came up to me, and dropping her novice curtsy, said, "Here's a ring, my lady, I found on the grass; they tell me it is yours, my lady!"

"No, my good girl, it is not mine," said I.

"It is Lady Leonora's," said Mr. L—.

At the sound of her name Leonora came forward.

The girl looked alternately at us.

"Can you doubt," cried Colonel A—, "which of these ladies is Mr. L—'s wife?"

"Oh, no, sir; this is she, to be sure," said the girl, pointing to me.

What there was in the girl's accent, or in L—'s look, when she pronounced the words, or in mine, or in all three together, I cannot exactly describe; but Leonora felt it. She turned as pale as death. I looked as unconscious as I could. L— went on fanning me, without seeing his wife's change of countenance. Leonora—would you believe it?—sank upon a bench behind us, and fainted. How her husband started, when he felt her catch by his arm as she fell! He threw down the fan, left me, ran for water—"Oh, Lady Leonora! Lady Leonora is ill!" exclaimed every voice. The consternation was wonderful. They carried her ladyship to a spot where she could have free air. I was absolutely in an instant left alone, and seemingly as much forgotten as if I had never existed! I was indeed so much astonished, that I could not stir from the place where I stood; till, recollecting myself, I pushed my way through the crowd, and came in view of Leonora just as she opened her eyes. As soon as she came to herself, she made an effort to stand, saying that she was quite well again, but that she would go into the house and repose herself for a few minutes. As she rose, a hundred arms were offered at once to her assistance. She stepped forward; and, to my surprise, and I believe to the surprise of every body else, took mine, made a sign to her husband not to follow us, and walked quickly towards the house. Her woman, with a face of terror, met us, as we were going into Lady Leonora's apartment, with salts and hartshorn, and I know not what in her hands.

"I am quite well, quite well again; I do not want any thing; I do not want any thing. I do not want you, Mason," said Leonora. "Lady Olivia is so good as to assist me. I am come in only to rest for a few minutes."

The woman gave me an evil look, and left the room. Never did I wish any thing more than that she should have stayed. I was absolutely so embarrassed, so distressed, when I found myself alone with Leonora, that I knew not what to say. I believe I began with a sentence about the night air, that was very little to the purpose. The sight of some baby-linen which the maid had been making suggested to me something which I thought more appropriate.

"My dear creature!" said I, "why will you fatigue yourself. so terribly, and stand so much and so long in your situation?"

Leonora neither accepted nor rejected my interpretation of what had passed. She made no reply; but fixed her eyes upon me as if she would have read my very soul. Never did I see or feel eyes so expressive or so powerful as hers were at this, moment. Mine absolutely fell beneath them. What deprived me of presence of mind I know not; but I was utterly without common sense. I am sure I changed colour, and Leonora must have seen it through my rouge, for I had only the slightest tinge upon my cheeks. The consciousness that she saw me blush disconcerted me beyond recovery; it is really quite unaccountable: I trembled all over as I stood before her; I was forced to have recourse to the hartshorn and water, which stood upon the table. Leonora rose, and threw open the window to give me fresh air. She pressed my hand, but rather with an air of forgiveness than of affection; I was mortified and vexed; but my pride revived me.

"We had better return to the company as soon as possible, I believe," said she, looking down at the moving crowd below.

"I am ready to attend you, my dear," said I, coldly, "whenever you feel yourself sufficiently rested and composed."

She left the room, and I followed. You have no idea of the solicitude with which the people hoped she was better—and well—and quite well, &c. What amazing importance a fainting fit can sometimes bestow! Her husband seemed no longer to have any eyes or soul but for her. At supper, and during the rest of the night, she occupied the whole attention of every body present. Can you conceive any thing so provoking? But L— must be an absolute fool!—Did he never see a woman faint before?—He cannot pretend to be in love with his wife—I do not understand it.—But this I know, that he has been totally different in his manner towards me these three days past.

And now that my curiosity is satisfied about Leonora's jealousy, I shall absolutely perish with ennui in this stupid place. Adieu, dearest Gabrielle! How I envy you! The void of my heart is insupportable. I must have some passion to keep me alive. Forward any letters from poor R—, if he has written under cover to you.

OLIVIA.

THE DUCHESS OF — TO HER DAUGHTER.

Take courage, my beloved daughter; take courage. Have a just confidence in yourself and in your husband. For a moment he may be fascinated by the arts of an unprincipled woman; for a moment she may triumph over his senses, and his imagination; but of his esteem, his affection, his heart, she cannot rob you. These have been, ought to be, will be yours. Trust to your mother's prophecy, my child. You may trust to it securely: for, well as she loves you—and no mother ever loved a daughter better—she does not soothe you with mere words of doting fondness; she speaks to you the language of reason and of truth.

I know what such a man as Mr. L— must esteem and love; I know of what such a woman as my daughter is capable, when her whole happiness, and the happiness of all that is dear to her, are at stake. The loss of temporary admiration and power, the transient preference shown to a despicable rival, will not provoke you to imprudent reproach, nor sink you to helpless despair. The arts of an Olivia might continue to deceive your husband, if he were a fool; or to please him, if he were a libertine: but he has a heart formed for love, he cannot therefore be a libertine: he is a man of superior abilities, and knows women too well to be a dupe. With a penetrating and discriminative judgment of character, he is a nice observer of female manners; his taste is delicate even to excess; under a cold exterior he has a vivid imagination and strong sensibility; he has little vanity, but a superabundance of pride; he wishes to be ardently loved, but this he conceals; it is difficult to convince him that he is beloved, and scarcely possible to satisfy him by any common proofs of attachment. A coquette will never attach Mr. L—. The admiration which others might express for her charms and accomplishments, would never pique him to competition: far from seeking "to win her praise whom all admire," he would disdain to enter the lists with the vulgar multitude: a heart, in which he had a probability of holding only divided empire, would not appear to him worth the winning. As a coquette, whatever may be her talents, graces, accomplishments, and address, you have nothing seriously to fear from Lady Olivia.

But, my dear, Mr. L—'s mind may be in a situation to require amusement. That species of apathy which succeeds to passion is not, as the inexperienced imagine, the death of love, but the necessary and salutary repose from which it awakens refreshed and revived. Mr. L—'s passion for you has been not only tender, but violent, and the calm, which inevitably succeeds, should not alarm you.

When a man feels that his fondness for a wife is suspended, he is uneasy in her company, not only from the sense of decreased pleasure, but from the fear of her observation and detection. If she reproach him, affairs become worse; he blames himself, he fears to give pain whenever he is in her presence: if he attempt to conceal his feelings, and to appear what he is no longer, a lover, his attempts are awkward; he becomes more and more dissatisfied with himself; and the person who compels him to this hypocrisy, who thus degrades him in his own eyes, must certainly be in danger of becoming an object of aversion. A wife, who has sense enough to abstain from all reproaches, direct or indirect, by word or look, may reclaim her husband's affections: the bird escapes from his cage, but returns to his nest. I am glad that you have agreeable company at your house; they will amuse Mr. L—, and relieve you from the necessity of taking a share in any conversation that you dislike. Our witty friend — will supply your share of conversation; and as to your silence, remember that witty people are always content with those who act audience.

I rejoice that you persist in your daily occupations. To a mind like yours, the sense of performing your duty will, next to religion, he the firmest support upon which you can rely.

Perhaps, my dear, even when you read this, you will still be inclined to justify Lady Olivia, and to conceal from your heart the suspicions which her conduct excites. I am not surprised, that you should find it difficult to believe, that one to whom you have behaved so generously, should treat you with treachery, and ingratitude. I am not surprised, that you who feel what it is to love, should think, that a woman whose heart is occupied by attachment to one object, must be incapable of thinking of any other. But love in such a heart as yours is totally different from what it is in the fancy of these heroines. In their imagination, the objects are as fleeting as the pictures in the clouds chased by the wind.

From Lady Olivia expect nothing: depend only on yourself. When you become, as you soon must, completely convinced that the woman, in whom your unsuspecting soul confided, is utterly unworthy of your esteem, refrain from all imprudent expressions of indignation. I despise—you will soon hate—your rival; but in the moment of detection think of what is due to yourself, and act as calmly as if you had never loved her. She will suffer no pain from the loss of your friendship: she has not a heart that can value it. Probably she is envious of you. All these women desire to mortify those whom they cannot degrade to their own level: and I am inclined to suspect that this malevolent feeling, joined to the want of occupation, may be the cause of her present conduct. Her manoeuvres will not ultimately succeed. She will be deserted by Mr. L—, disappointed and disgraced, and your husband will be more yours than ever. When this happy moment comes, my Leonora; when your husband returns, preferring yours to all other society, then will be the time to exert all your talents, all your charms, to prove your superiority in every thing, but most in love. The soothings of female tenderness, in certain situations, have power not only to calm the feelings of self-reproach, but to diffuse delight over the soul of man. The oil, which the skilful mariner throws upon the sea, not only smooths the waves in the storm, but when the sun shines, spreads the most beautiful colours over the surface of the waters.

My dear daughter, though your mother writes seemingly at her ease, you must not fancy that she does not feel for you. Do not imagine, that in the coldness of extinguished passions, and in the pride of counselling age, your mother expects to charm agony with words. No, my child, I am not so absurd, so cruel. Your letter forced tears from eyes, which are not used like sentimental eyes to weep upon every trifling occasion. My first wish was to set out immediately to see you; but whatever consolation or pleasure my company might afford, I believe it might be disadvantageous to you in your present circumstances. I could not be an hour in the room with this Lady Olivia, without showing some portion of the indignation and contempt that I feel for her conduct. This warmth of mine might injure you in your husband's opinion. Though you would have too strong a sense of propriety, and too much dignity of mind, to make complaints of your husband to me, or to any one living; yet it might be supposed that your mother was your confidante in secret, and your partisan in public: this might destroy your domestic happiness. No husband can or ought to endure the idea of his wife's caballing against him. I admire and shall respect your dignified silence.

And now fare you well, my dearest child. May God bless you! If a mother's prayers could avail, you would be the happiest of human beings. I do, without partiality, believe you to be one of the best and most amiable of women.

LETTER XXVIII

LEONORA TO HER MOTHER.

Had your letter, my dearest mother, reached me a few hours sooner, I should not have exposed myself as I have done.

Yesterday, at our fête champêtre, you would have been ashamed of me. I am ashamed of myself. I did the very reverse of what I ought, of what I would have done, if I had been fortified by your counsel. Instead of being calm and dignified, I was agitated beyond all power of control. I lost all presence of mind, all common sense, all recollection.

I know your contempt for swooning heroines. What will you say, when you hear that your daughter fainted—fainted in public? I believe, however, that, as soon as I recovered, I had sufficient command over myself to prevent the accident from being attributed to the real cause, and I hope that the very moment I came to my recollection, my manner towards Lady Olivia was such as to preclude all possibility of her being blamed or even suspected. From living much abroad, she has acquired a certain freedom of manner, and latitude of thinking, which expose her to suspicion; but of all serious intention to injure me, or to pass the bounds of propriety, I totally acquit her. She is not to blame for the admiration she excites, nor is she to be the sufferer for my weakness of mind or of health.

Great and unreasonable folly I am sure I showed—but I shall do so no more.

The particular circumstances I need not explain: you may be assured, that wherever I think it right to be silent, nothing shall tempt me to speak: but I understood, by the conclusion of your letter, that you expect me to preserve an absolute silence upon this subject in future: this I will not promise. I cannot conceive that I, who do not mean to injure any human being, ought, because I am unhappy, and when I am most in want of a friend, to be precluded from the indulgence of speaking of what is nearest my heart to that dear, safe, most enlightened, and honourable of friends, who has loved, guided, instructed, and encouraged me in every thing that is right from my infancy. Why should I be refused all claim to sympathy? why must my thoughts and feelings be shut up in my own breast? and why must I be a solitary being, proscribed from commerce with my own family, with my beloved mother, to whom I have been accustomed to tell every feeling and idea as they arose? No; to all that is honourable I will strictly conform; but, by the superstition of prudence, I do not hold myself bound.

Nothing could be kinder than my husband's conduct to me the evening after I was taken ill. He left home early this morning; he is gone to meet his friend, General B—, who has just returned from abroad. I hope that Mr. L— will be absent only a few days; for it would be fatal to my happiness if he should find amusement at a distance from home. His home, at all events, shall never be made a cage to him; when he returns, I will exert myself to the utmost to make it agreeable. This I hope can be done without obtruding my company upon him, or putting myself in competition with any person. I could wish that some fortunate accident might induce Lady Olivia to leave us before Mr. L—'s return. Had I the same high opinion of her generosity that I once formed, had I the same perfect confidence in her integrity and in her friendship for me, I would go this moment and tell her all that passes in my heart: no humiliation of my vanity would cost me any thing if it could serve the interests of my love; no mean pride could stand in my mind against the force of affection. But there is a species of pride which I cannot, will not renounce—believing, as I do, that it is the companion, the friend, the support of virtue. This pride, I trust, will never desert me: it has grown with my growth; it was implanted in my character by the education which my dear mother gave me; and now, even by her, it cannot be eradicated. Surely I have misunderstood one passage in your letter: you cannot advise your daughter to restrain just indignation against vice from any motive of policy or personal interest. You say to me, "In the moment of detection think of what is due to yourself, and act as calmly as if you had never loved her." If I could, I would not do this. Contempt shown by virtue is the just punishment of vice, a punishment which no selfish consideration should mitigate. If I were convinced that Lady Olivia were guilty, would you have me behave to her as if I believed her to be innocent? My countenance, my voice, my principles, would revolt from such mean and pernicious hypocrisy, degrading to the individual, and destructive to society.

May I never more see the smile of love on the lips of my husband, nor its expression in his eyes, if I do so degrade myself in my own opinion and in his! Yes, in his; for would not he, would not any man of sense or delicacy, recur to that idea so common with his sex, and so just, that if a woman will sacrifice her sense of honour to her passions in one instance, she may in another? Would he not argue, "If she will do this for me because she is in love with me, why not for a new favourite, if time or accident should make me less an object of passion?" No; I may lose his love—this would he my misfortune: but to forfeit his esteem would be my fault; and, under the remorse which I should then have to endure, I am persuaded that no power of art or nature could sustain my existence.

So much for myself. As to the general good of society, that, I confess, is not at this moment the uppermost consideration in my mind; but I will add a few words on that subject, lest you should imagine me to be hurried away by my own feelings. Public justice and reason are, I think, on my side. What would become of the good order of society or the decency of families, if every politic wife were to receive or invite, or permit her husband's mistress to reside in her house? What would become of conjugal virtue in either sex, if the wife were in this manner not only to connive at the infidelity of her husband, but to encourage and provide for his inconsistency? If she enters into bonds of amity and articles of partnership with her rival, with that person by whom she has been most injured, instead of being the dignified sufferer, she becomes an object of contempt.

My dearest mother, my most respected friend, my sentiments on this subject cannot essentially differ from yours. I must have mistaken your meaning. Pray write quickly, and tell me so; and forgive, if you cannot approve of, the warmth with which I have spoken.

I am your truly affectionate

And grateful daughter,

LEONORA L—

LETTER XXIX

OLIVIA TO MADAME P—.

My amiable Gabrielle, I must be faithful to my promise of writing to you every week, though this place affords nothing new either in events or sentiment. Mr. L—'s absence made this castle insupportably dull. A few days ago he returned home, and met me with an easy kind of indifference, provoking enough to a woman who has been accustomed to excite some sensation. However, I was rejoiced at this upon Leonora's account. She was evidently delighted, and her spirits and affections seemed to overflow involuntarily upon all around her; even to me her manner became quite frank and cordial, almost caressing. She is really handsome when she is animated, and her conversation this evening quite surprised me. I saw something of that playfulness, those light touches, that versatility of expression, those words that mean more than meet the ear; every thing, in short, that could charm in the most polished foreign society. Leonora seemed to be inspired with all the art of conversation, by the simple instinct of affection. What astonished me most was the grace with which she introduced some profound philosophical remarks. "Such pearls," said Mr. L—, "come from the deep."

With all these talents, what might not Leonora be in proper hands! But now she is nothing except to her husband, and a few intimate friends. However, this is not my affair. Let me go on to what concerns myself. You may believe, my dear Gabrielle, that I piqued myself upon showing at least as much easy indifference as was shown to me: freedom encourages freedom. As there was no danger of my being too amiable, I did not think myself bound in honour or sentiment to keep myself in the shade; but I could not be as brilliant as you have seen me at your soirees: the magic circle of adorers, the inspiring power of numbers, the éclat of public representation, were wanting. I retired to my own apartment at night, quite out of humour with myself; and Josephine, as she undressed me, put me still further out of patience, by an ill-timed history of a dispute she has had with Leonora's Swiss servant. The Swiss and Josephine, it seems, came to high words in defence of their mistresses' charms. Josephine provoked the Swiss by saying, that his lady might possibly be handsome if she were dressed in the French taste; mais qu'elle étoit bien Angloise, and would be quite another thing if she had been at Paris. The Swiss retorted by observing, that Josephine's lady had indeed learnt in perfection at Paris the art of making herself up, which was quite necessary to a beauty un peu passée. The words were not more agreeable to me than they had been to Josephine. I wonder at her assurance in repeating them—"Un peu passée!" Many a woman in England, ten, fifteen years older than I am, has inspired a violent passion; and it has been observed, that power is retained by these mature charmers, longer than conquest can be preserved by inexperienced beauties. There are women who have learnt to combine, for their own advantage, and for that of their captives, all the pleasure and conveniences of society, all that a thorough knowledge of the world can give—women who have a sufficient attention to appearances, joined to a real contempt of all prejudices, especially that of constancy—women who possess that knowledge of the human heart, which well compensates transient bloom; who add the expression of sentiment to beautiful features, and who employ

"Gay smiles to comfort, April showers to move, And all the nature, all the art of Love."

—"Un peu passée!" The Swiss is impertinent, and knows nothing of the matter. His master knows but little more. He would, however, know infinitely more if I could take the trouble to instruct him; to which I am almost tempted for want of something better to do. Adieu, my Gabrielle. R—'s silence is perfectly incomprehensible.

OLIVIA.

LETTER XXX

OLIVIA TO MADAME DE P—.

So, my amiable Gabrielle, you are really interested in my letters, though written during my English exile, and you are curious to know whether any of my potent spells can wake into life this man of marble. I candidly confess you would inspire me with an ambition to raise my poor countrymen in your opinion, if I were not restrained by the sacred sentiment of friendship, which forbids me to rival Leonora even in a husband's opinion.

However, Josephine, who feels herself a party concerned ever since her battle with the Swiss, has piqued herself upon dressing me with exquisite taste. I am every day mise à ravir!—and with such perfection of art, that no art appears—all is negligent simplicity. I let Josephine please herself; for you know I am not bound to be frightful, because I have a friend whose husband may chance to turn his eye upon my figure, when he is tired of admiring hers. I rallied L— the other day upon his having no eyes or ears but for his wife. Be assured I did it in such a manner that he could not be angry. Then I went on to a comparison between the facility of French and English society. He admitted that there was some truth and more wit in my observations. I was satisfied. With these reasonable men, the grand point for a woman is to amuse them—they can have logic from their own sex. But, my Gabrielle, I am summoned to the salon, and must finish my letter another day.

Heaven! can it be a fortnight since I wrote a line to my Gabrielle!—Where was I?—"With these reasonable men the grand point for a woman is to amuse them." True—most true! L—, believing himself only amused with my lively nonsense, indulged himself with it continually. I was to believe only what he believed. Presently he could not do without my conversation for more than two hours together. What was I to do, my Gabrielle? I walked out to avoid him. He found me in the woods—rallied me on my taste for solitude, and quoted Voltaire.

This led to a metaphysical conversation, half playful, half serious:—the distinction which a man sometimes makes to his conscience between thinking a woman entertaining, and feeling her interesting, vanishes more easily, and more rapidly, than he is aware of—at least in certain situations. This was not an observation I could make to my companion in the woods, and he certainly did not make it for himself. It would have been vanity in me to have broken off our conversation, lest he should fall in love with me—it would have been blindness not to have seen that he was in some danger. I thought of Leonora— and sighed—and did all that was in my power to put him upon his guard. By way of preservative, I frankly made him a confession of my attachment to R—. This I imagined would put things upon a right footing for ever; but, on the contrary, by convincing him of my innocence, and of my having no designs on his heart, this candour has, I fear, endangered him still more; yet I know not what to think—his manner is so variable towards me—I must be convinced of what his sentiments are, before I can decide what my conduct ought to be. Adieu, my amiable Gabrielle; I wait for something decisive with an inexpressible degree of anxiety—I will not now call it curiosity.—Apropos, does R— wish that I should forget that he exists? What is this business that detains him? But why do I condescend to inquire?

OLIVIA.

LETTER XXXI

GENERAL B— TO MR. L—.

MY DEAR L—, London.

I send you the horse to which you took a fancy. He has killed one of his grooms, and lamed two; but you will be his master, and I hope he will know it.

I have a word to say to you on a more serious subject. Pardon me if I tell you that I think you are a happy man, and excuse me if I add, that if you do not keep yourself so I shall not think you a wise one. A good wife is better than a good-for-nothing mistress.—A self-evident proposition!—A stupid truism! Yes; but if every man who knows a self-evident proposition when he sees it on paper, always acted as if he knew it, this would be a very wise and a very happy world; and I should not have occasion to write this letter.

You say that you are only amusing yourself at the expense of a finished coquette; take care that she does not presently divert herself at yours.—"You are proof against French coquetry and German sentiment."—Granted—but a fine woman?—and your own vanity?—But you have no vanity.—You call it pride then, I suppose. I will not quarrel with you for a name. Pride, properly managed, will do your business as well as vanity. And no doubt Lady Olivia knows this as well as I do. I hope you may never know it better.

I am, my dear friend,

Truly yours,

J. B.

LETTER XXXII

OLIVIA TO MADAME DE P—.

L— Castle.

Advise me, dearest Gabrielle; I am in a delicate situation; and on your judgment and purity of heart I have the most perfect reliance. Know, then, that I begin to believe that Leonora's jealousy was not so absolutely absurd as I at first supposed. She understood her husband better than I did. I begin to fear that I have made a serious impression whilst I meant only to amuse myself. Heaven is my witness, I simply intended to satisfy my curiosity, and that once gratified, it was my determination to respect the weakness I discovered. To love Leonora, as once I imagined I could, is out of my power; but to disturb her peace, to destroy her happiness, to make use of the confidence she has reposed in me, the kindness she has shown by making me an inmate of her house—my soul shudders at these ideas. No—if her husband really loves me I will fly. Leonora shall see that Olivia is incapable of treachery—that Olivia has a soul generous and delicate as her own, though free from the prejudices by which she is fettered. To Leonora a husband is a lover—I shall consider him as such, and respect her property. You are so little used, my dear Gabrielle, to consider a husband in this point of view, that you will scarcely enter into my feelings: but put yourself in my situation, allow for nationality of principle, and I am persuaded you would act as I shall. Spare me your raillery; seriously, if Leonora's husband is in love with me, would you not advise me, my dearest friend, to fly him, "far as pole from pole?" Write to me, I conjure you, my Gabrielle—write instantly, and tell me whether R— is now at Paris. I will return thither immediately if you advise it. My mind is in such confusion, I have no power to decide; I will be guided by your advice.

OLIVIA.

MADAME DE P— TO OLIVIA.

Paris.

Advice! my charming Olivia! do you ask me for advice? I never gave or took advice in my life, except for les vapeurs noirs. And your understanding is so far superior to mine, and you comprehend the characters of these English so much better than I do, that I cannot pretend to counsel you. This Lady Leonora is inconceivable with her passion for her own husband; but how ridiculous to let it be suspected! If her heart is so tender, cannot she, with all her charms, find a lover on whom to bestow it, without tormenting that poor Mr. L—? Evidently he is tired of her: and I am sure I should be worn to death were I in his place. Nothing so tiresome as love without mystery, and without obstacles. And this must ever be the case with conjugal love. Eighteen months married, I think you say, and Lady Leonora expects her husband to be still at her feet! And she wishes it! Truly she is the most unreasonable woman upon earth—and the most extraordinary; but I am tired of thinking of what I cannot comprehend.

Let us pass on to Mr. L—. By your last letters, I should judge that he might be an agreeable man, if his wife were out of the question. Matrimonial jealousy is a new idea to me; I can judge of it only by analogy. In affairs of gallantry, I have sometimes seen one of the parties continue to love when the other has become indifferent, and then they go on tormenting one another and being miserable, because they have not the sense to see that a fire cannot be made of ashes. Sometimes I have found romantic young people persuade themselves that they can love no more because they can love one another no longer; but if they had sufficient courage to say—I am tired—and I cannot help it—they would come to a right understanding immediately, and part on the best terms possible; each eager to make a new choice, and to be again in love and happy. All this to be done with decency, of course. And if there be no scandal, where is the harm? Can it signify to the universe whether Mons. Un tel likes Madame Une telle or Madame Une autre? Provided there is love enough, all the world is in good humour, and that is the essential point; for without good humour, what becomes of the pleasures of society? As to the rest, I think of inconstancy, or infidelity, as it is called, much as our good La Fontaine did—"Quand on le sait, c'est peu de chose—quand on ne le sait pas, ce n'est rien."

To promise to love one person eternally! What a terrible engagement! It freezes my heart even to think of it. I am persuaded, that if I were bound to love him for life, I should detest the most amiable man upon earth in ten minutes—a husband more especially. Good heavens! how I should abhor M. de P— if I saw him in this point of view! On the contrary, now I love him infinitely—that is to say, as one loves a husband. I have his interest at heart, and his glory. When I thought he was going to prison I was in despair. I was at home to no one but Brave-et-Tendre, and to him only to consult on the means of obtaining my husband's pardon. M. de P— is sensible of this, and on my part I have no reason to complain of his liberality. We are perfectly happy, though we meet perhaps but for a few minutes in the day; and is not this better than tiring one another for four-and-twenty hours? When I grow old—if ever I do—he will be my best friend. In the mean time I support his credit with all my influence. This very morning I concluded an affair for him, which never could have succeeded, if the intimate friend of the minister had not been also my lover. Now, why cannot your Lady Leonora and her Mr. L— live on the same sort of terms? But if English manners will not permit of this, I have nothing more to say. Above all things a woman must respect opinion, else she cannot be well received in the world. I conclude this is the secret of Lady Leonora's conduct. But then jealousy!—no woman, I suppose, is bound, even in England, to be jealous in order to show her love for her husband. I lose myself again in trying to understand what is incomprehensible.

As to you, my dear Olivia, you also amaze me by talking of crimes and horror, and flying from pole to pole to avoid a man because you have made him at last find out that he has a heart! You have done him the greatest possible service: it may preserve him perhaps from hanging himself next November—that month in which, according to Voltaire's philosophical calendar, Englishmen always hang themselves, because the atmosphere is so thick, and their ennui so heavy. Lady Leonora, if she really loves her husband, ought to be infinitely obliged to you for averting this danger. As to the rest, your heart is not concerned, so you can have nothing to fear; and as for a platonic attachment on the part of Mr. L—, his wife, even according to her own rigid principles, cannot blame you.

Adieu, my charming friend! Instead of laughing at your fit of prudery, I ought to encourage your scruples, that I might profit by them. If they should bring you to Paris immediately, with what joy should I embrace my Olivia, and how much gratitude should I owe to the jealousy of Lady Leonora L—!

R— is not yet returned. When I have any news to give you of him, depend upon it you shall hear from me again. Accept, my interesting Olivia, the vows of my most tender and eternal friendship.

GABRIELLE DE P—.

OLIVIA TO MADAME DE P—.

L— Castle, Tuesday.

Your charming letter, my Gabrielle, has at once revived my spirits and dissipated all my scruples; you mistake, however, in supposing that Leonora is in love with her husband: more and more reason have I every hour to be convinced that Leonora has never known the passion of love; consequently her jealousy was, as I at first pronounced it to be, the selfish jealousy of matrimonial power and property. Else why does it subside, why does it vanish, when, if it were a jealousy of the heart, it has now more provocation, infinitely more than when it appeared in full force? Leonora could see that her husband distinguished me at a fête champêtre; she could see what the eyes of others showed her; she could hear what envy whispered, or what scandal hinted; she was mortified, she was alarmed even to fainting by a public preference, by a silly country girl's mistaking me for the wife, and doing homage to me as to the lady of the manor; but Leonora cannot perceive in the object of her affection the symptoms that mark the rise and progress of a real love. Leonora feels not the little strokes, which would be fatal blows to the peace of a truly delicate mind; she heeds not "the trifles light as air" which would be confirmation strong to a soul of genuine sensibility. My influence over the mind of L— increases rapidly, and I shall let it rise to its acme before I seem to notice it. Leonora, re-assured, I suppose, by a few flattering words, and more, perhaps, by an exalted opinion of her own merit, has lately appeared quite at her ease, and blind to all that passes before her eyes. It is not for me to dissipate this illusion prematurely—it is not for me to weaken this confidence in her husband. To an English wife this would be death. Let her foolish security then last as long as possible. After all, how much anguish of heart, how many pangs of conscience, how much of the torture of pity, am I spared by this callous temper in my friend! I may indulge in a little harmless coquetry, without danger to her peace, and without scruple, enjoy the dear possession of power.

"Say, for you know," charming Gabrielle, what is the delight of obtaining power over the human heart? Let the lords of the creation boast of their power to govern all things; to charm these governors be ours. Let the logicians of the earth boast their power to regulate the world by reason; be it ours, Gabrielle, to intoxicate and humble proud reason to the dust beneath our feet.—And who shall blame in us this ardour for universal dominion? If they are men, I call them tyrants—if they are women, I call them hypocrites—and the two vices which I most detest are tyranny and hypocrisy. Frankly I confess, that I feel in all its restless activity the passion for general admiration. I cannot conceive—can you, Gabrielle, a pleasure more transporting than the perception of extended and extending dominion? The struggle of the rebel heart for freedom makes the war more tempting, the victory more glorious, the triumph more splendid. Secure of your sympathy, ma belle Gabrielle, I shall not fear to tire you by my commentaries.

Male coquetry justifies female retaliation to any imaginable extent. Upon this principle, on which I have seen you act so often, and so successfully, I shall now intrepidly proceed. This man makes a show of resistance; be it at his own peril: he thinks that he is gaining power over my heart, whilst I am preparing torments for his; he fancies that he is throwing chains round me, whilst I am rivetting fetters from which he will in vain attempt to escape. He is proud, and has the insanity of desiring to be exclusively beloved, yet affects to set no value upon the preference that is shown to him; appears satisfied with his own approbation, and stoically all-sufficient to his own happiness. Leonora does not know how to manage his temper, but I do. The suspense, however, in which he keeps me is tantalizing: he shall pay for it hereafter: I had no idea, till lately, that he had so much self-command. At times he has actually made me doubt my own power. At certain moments I have been half tempted to believe that I had made no serious impression, that he had been only amusing himself at my expense, and for Leonora's gratification: but upon careful and cool observation I am convinced that his indifference is affected, that all his stoicism will prove vain. The arrow is lodged in his heart, and he must fall, whether he turn upon the enemy in anger, or fly in dismay.

My pride is exasperated. I am not accustomed to such obstinate resistance. I really almost hate this invincible man, and—strange inconsistency of the human heart!—almost love him. Heaven and pride preserve me from such a weakness! But there is certainly something that piques and stimulates one's feelings in this species of male coquetry. L— understands the business better than I thought he could. One moment my knowledge of the arts of his sex puts me on my guard; the next my sensibility exposes me in the most terrible manner. Experience ought to protect me, but it only shows me the peril and my inability to escape. Ah! Gabrielle, without a heart how safe we should be, how dangerous to our lovers! But cursed with sensibility, we must, alas! submit to our fate. The habit of loving, le besoin d'aimer, is more powerful than all sense of the folly and the danger. Nor is the tempest of the passions so dreadful as the dead calm of the soul. Why did R— suffer my soul to sink into this ominous calm? The fault is his; let him abide the consequences. Why did he not follow me to England? why did he not write to me? or when he did write, why were his letters so cold, so spiritless? When I spoke of divorce, why did he hesitate? Why did he reason when he should have only felt? Tell him, my tender, my delicate friend, these are questions which the heart asks, and which the heart only can answer. Adieu.

OLIVIA.

LETTER XXXV

MADAME DE P— TO OLIVIA.

Paris.

Je suis excede! mon coeur. Alive, and but just alive, after such a day of fatigues! All morning from one minister to another! then home to my toilette! then a great dinner with a number of foreigners, each to be distinguished—then au Feydeau, where I was obliged to go to support poor S—'s play. It would be really insupportable, if it were not for the finest music in the world, which, after all, the French music certainly is. There was a violent party against the piece; and we were so late, that it was just on the point of perishing. My ears have not yet recovered from the horrid noise. In the midst of the tumult I happily, by a master-stroke, turned the fortune of the night. I spied the shawl of an English woman hanging over the box. This, you know, like scarlet to the bull, is sufficient to enrage the Parisian pit. To the shawl I directed the fury of the mob of critics. Luckily for us, the lady was attended only by an Englishman, who of course chose to assert his right not to understand the customs of any country, or submit to any will but his own. He would not permit the shawl to be stirred. A bas! à bas: resounded from below. The uproar was inconceivable. You would have thought that the house must have come down. In the mean time the piece went on, and the shawl covered all its defects. Admire my generalship. T— tells me I was born for a general; yet I rather think my forte is negotiation.

But I have not yet come to your affairs, for which alone I could undergo the fatigue of writing at this moment. Guess, my Olivia, what apparition I met at the door of my box to-night. But the enclosed note will save you the trouble of guessing. I could not avoid permitting him to slide his billet-doux into my hand as he put on my shawl. Adieu. I must refuse myself the pleasure of conversing longer with my sweet friend. Fresh toils await me. Madame la Grande will never forgive me if I do not appear for a moment at her soiree: and la petite Q— will be jealous beyond recovery, if I do not give her a moment: and it is Madame R—'s night. There I must be; for all the ambassadors, as usual, will be there; and as some of them, I have reason to believe, go on purpose to meet me, I cannot disappoint their Excellencies. My friends would never forgive it. I am positively quite weary of this life of eternal bustle; but once in the eddy, one is carried round and round; there is no stopping. Adieu, adieu. I write under the hands of Victoire. O that she had your taste to guide her, and to decide my too vacillating judgment! we should then have no occasion to dread even the elegant simplicity of Madame R—'s toilette.

GABRIELLE DE P—.

LETTER XXXVI

OLIVIA TO MADAME DE F—.

My Gabrielle, I have read R—'s note enclosed in your charming sprightly letter. What a contrast! So cold! so formal! A thousand times rather would I not have heard from him, than have received a letter so little in unison with my feelings. He talks to me of business. Business! What business ought to detain a man a moment from the woman he loves? The interests of his ambition are nothing to me. What are all these to love? Is he so mean as to hesitate between them? then I despise him! and Olivia can never love the being she despises!

Does R— flatter himself that his power over my heart is omnipotent? Does he imagine that Olivia is to be slighted with impunity? Does R— think that a woman, who has even nominally the honour to reign over his heart, cannot meditate new conquests? Oh, credulous vanity of man! He fancies, perhaps, that he is secure of the maturer age of one, who fondly devoted to him her inexperienced youth. "Security is the curse of fools." Does he in his wisdom deem a woman's age a sufficient pledge for her constancy? He might every day see examples enough to convince him of his error. In fact, the age of women has nothing to do with the number of their years. Possibly, however, the gallant gentleman may be of opinion with Leonora's Swiss, that Lady Olivia is un peu passé. Adieu, my dear friend; you, who always understand and sympathize in my feelings, you will express them for me in the best manner possible. I shall not write to R—. You will see him; and Olivia commits to you what to a woman of delicacy is more dear than her love—her just resentment.

OLIVIA.

LETTER XXXVII

OLIVIA TO MADAME DE P—.

L— Castle.

Pity me, dearest Gabrielle, for I am in need of all the pity which your susceptible heart can bestow. Never was woman in such a terrible situation! Yes, Gabrielle, this provoking, this incomprehensible, this too amiable man, has entangled your poor friend past recovery. Her sentiments and sensations must henceforward be in eternal opposition to each other. Friendship, gratitude, honour, virtue, all in tremendous array, forbid her to think of love; but love, imperious love, will not be so defied: he seizes upon his victim, and now, as in all the past, will be the ruler, the tyrant of Olivia's destiny. Never was confusion, amazement, terror, remorse, equal to mine, Gabrielle, when I first discovered that I loved him. Who could have foreseen, who could have imagined it? I meant but to satisfy an innocent curiosity, to indulge harmless coquetry, to gratify the natural love of admiration, and to enjoy the possession of power. Alas! I felt not that, whilst I was acquiring ascendancy over the heart of another, I was beguiled of all command over my own. I flattered myself that, when honour should bid me stop, I could pause without hesitation, without effort: I promised myself, that the moment I should discover that I was loved by the husband of my friend I should fly from him for ever. Alas! it is no longer time—to fly from him is no longer in my power. Oh. Gabrielle! I love him: he knows that I love him. Never did woman suffer more than I have done since I wrote to you last. The conflict was too violent for my feeble frame. I have been ill—very ill: a nervous fever brought me nearly to the grave. Why did I not die? I should have escaped the deep humiliation, the endless self-reproach to which my future existence is doomed.— Leonora!—Why do I start at that name? Oh! there is horror in the sound! Even now perhaps she knows and triumphs in my weakness. Even now, perhaps, her calm insensible soul blesses itself for not being made like mine. Even now perhaps her husband doubts whether he shall accept Olivia's love, or sacrifice your wretched friend to Leonora's pride. Oh, Gabrielle, no words can describe what I suffer! But I must be calm, and explain the progress of this fatal passion. Explain—Heavens! how shall I explain what I cannot recollect without heart-rending anguish and confusion! Oh, Gabrielle! pity

Your distracted

OLIVIA.

LETTER XXXVIII

MADAME DE P— TO OLIVIA.

Monday.

My dear romantic Olivia! you must have a furious passion for tormenting yourself, when you can find matter for despair in your present situation. In your place I should rejoice to find that in the moment an old passion had consumed itself, a new one, fresh and vigorous, springs from its ashes. My charming friend, understand your own interests, and do not be the dupe of those fine phrases that we are obliged to employ to deceive others. Rail at Cupid as much as you please to the men in public, par façon; but always remember for your private use, that love is essential to our existence in society. What is a woman when she neither loves nor is loved? a mere personage muet in the drama of life. Is it not from our lovers that we derive our consequence? Even a beauty without lovers is but a queen without subjects. A woman who renounces love is an abdicated sovereign, always longing to resume her empire when it is too late; continually forgetting herself, like the pseudo-philosophic Christina, talking and acting as though she had still the power of life and death in her hands; a tyrant without guards or slaves; a most awkward, pitiable, and ridiculous personage. No, my fair Olivia, let us never abjure love; even when the reign of beauty passes away, that of grace and sentiment remains. As much delicacy as you please: without delicacy there is no grace, and without a veil, beauty loses her most captivating charms. I pity you, my dear, for having let your veil be blown aside malheureusement. But such accidents will happen. Who can control the passions or the winds? After all, l'erreur d'un moment is not irretrievable, and you reproach yourself too bitterly, my sweet friend, for your involuntary injustice to Lady Leonora. Assuredly it could not be your intention to sacrifice your repose to Mr. L—. You loved him against your will, did you not? And it is, you know, by the intention that we must judge of actions: the positive harm done to the world in general is in all cases the only just measure of criminality. Now what harm is done to the universe, and what injury can accrue to any individual, provided you keep your own counsel? As long as your friend is deceived, she is happy; it therefore becomes your duty, your virtue, to dissemble. I am no great casuist, but all this appears to me self-evident; and these I always thought were your principles of philosophy. My dear Olivia, I have drawn out my whole store of metaphysics with some difficulty for your service; I flatter myself I have set your poor distracted head to rights. One word more—for I like to go to the bottom of a subject, when I can do so in two minutes: virtue is desirable because it makes us happy; consequently, to make ourselves happy is to be truly virtuous. Methinks this is sound logic.

To tell you the truth, my dear Olivia, I do not well conceive how you have contrived to fall in love with this half-frozen Englishman. 'Tis done, however—there is no arguing against facts; and this is only one proof more of what I have always maintained, that destiny is inevitable and love irresistible. Voltaire's charming inscription on the statue of Cupid is worth all the volumes of reasoning and morality that ever were or ever will be written. Banish melancholy thoughts, my dear friend; they serve no manner of purpose but to increase your passion. Repentance softens the heart; and every body knows, that what softens the heart disposes it more to love: for which reason I never abandon myself to this dangerous luxury of repentance. Mon Dieu! why will people never benefit by experience? And to what purpose do they read history? Was not La Valliere ever penitent, and ever transgressing? ever in transports or in tears? You, at all events, my Olivia, can never become a Carmelite or a Magdalen. You have emancipated yourself from superstition: but whilst you ridicule all religious orders, do not inflict upon yourself their penances. The habit of some of the orders has been thought becoming. The modest costume of a nun is indeed one of the prettiest dresses one can wear at a masquerade ball, and it might even be worn without a mask, if it were fashionable: but nothing that is not fashionable can be becoming.

Adieu, my adorable Olivia: I will send you, by the first opportunity, your Lyons gown, which is really charming.

GABRIELLE DE P—.

LETTER XXXIX

OLIVIA TO MADAME DE P—.

Nov. 30th, —

Your truly philosophical letter, my infinitely various Gabrielle, infused a portion of its charming spirit into my soul. My mind was fortified and elevated by your eloquence. Who could think that a woman of such a lively genius could be so profound? and who could expect from a woman who has passed her life in the world, such original and deep reflections? You see you were mistaken when you thought that you had no genius for philosophic subjects.

After all that has been said by metaphysicians about the existence and seat of the moral sense, I think I can solve every difficulty by a new theory. You know some philosophers suppose the moral sense to be intuitive and inherent in man: others who deny the doctrine of innate ideas, treat this notion of innate sentiments as equally absurd. There they certainly are wrong, for sentiments are widely different from ideas, and I have that within me which convinces my understanding that sentiments must be innate, and proportioned to the delicacy of our sensibility; no person of common sense or feeling can doubt this. But there are other points which I own puzzled me till yesterday: some metaphysicians would seat the moral sense inherently in the heart, others would place it intuitively in the brain, all would confine it to the soul; now in my opinion it resides primarily and principally in the nerves, and varies with their variations. Hence the difficulty of making the moral sense a universal guide of action, since it not only differs in many individuals, but in the same persons at different periods of their existence, or (as I have often experienced) at different hours of the day. All this must depend upon the mobility of the nervous system: upon this may hinge the great difficulties which have puzzled metaphysicians respecting consciousness, identity, &c. If they had attended less to the nature of the soul, and more to the system of the nerves, they would have avoided innumerable errors, and probably would have made incalculably important discoveries. Nothing is wanting but some great German genius to bring this idea of a moral sense in the nerves into fashion. Indeed, if our friend Mad. — would mention it in the notes to her new novel, it would introduce it, in the most satisfactory manner possible, to all the fashionable world abroad; and we take our notions in this country implicitly from the continent. As for you, my dear Gabrielle, I know you cut the Gordian knot at once, by referring, with your favourite moralist, every principle of human nature to self-love. This does not quite accord with my ideas; there is something harsh in it that is repugnant to my sensibility; but you have a stronger mind than I have, and perhaps your theory is right.

"You tell me I contradict myself continually," says the acute and witty Duke de la Rochefoucault: "No, but the human heart, of which I treat, is in perpetual contradiction to itself." Permit me to avail myself of this answer, dear Gabrielle, if you should accuse me of contradicting in this letter all that I said to you in my last. A few hours after I had despatched it, the state of my nerves changed; I saw things of course in a new light, and repented having exposed myself to your raillery by writing in such a Magdalen strain. My nerves were more in fault than I. When one's mind, or one's nerves grow weak, the early associations and old prejudices of the nursery recur, and tyrannize over one's reason: from this evil your liberal education and enviable temperament have preserved you; but have charity for my feminine weakness of frame, which too often counteracts the masculine strength of my soul. Now that I have deprecated your ridicule for my last nervous nonsense, I will go on in a more rational manner. However my better judgment might have been clouded for a moment, I have recovered strength of mind enough to see that I am in no way to blame for any thing that has happened. If a man is amiable, and if I have taste and sensibility, I must see and feel it. "To love," as I remember your friend G— once finely observed to you, "to love, is a crime only in the eyes of demons, or of priests, who resemble demons." This is a general proposition, to which none but the prejudiced can refuse their assent: and what is true in general, must be true in particular. The accident, I use the term philosophically, not popularly, the accident of a man's being married, or, in other words, having entered imprudently into a barbarous and absurd civil contract, cannot alter the nature of things. The essence of truth cannot be affected by the variation of external circumstances. Now the proper application of metaphysics frees the mind from vulgar prejudices, and dissipates the baby terrors of an ill-educated conscience. To fall in love with a married man, and the husband of your intimate friend! How dreadful this sounds to some ears! even mine were startled at first, till I called reason to my assistance. Then I had another difficulty to combat—to own, and own unasked, a passion to the object of it, would shock the false delicacy of those who are governed by common forms, and who are slaves to vulgar prejudices: but a little philosophy liberates our sex from the tyranny of custom, teaches us to disdain hypocrisy, and to glory in the simplicity of truth.

Josephine had been perfuming my hair, and I was sitting reading at my toilette; the door of my dressing-room happened to be half open; L— was crossing the gallery, and as he passed I suppose his eye was caught by my hair, or perhaps he paused a moment, I am not certain how it was—my eyes were on my book.

"Ah! vous avez raison, monsieur, c'est la plus belle chevelure! Mais entrez donc, monsieur," cried Josephine, whom I can never teach to comprehend or respect English customs, "Eh! entrez, entrez, monsieur; madame est e sa toilette."

As I looked up I could not forbear smiling at the extreme ease and decision of Josephine's manner, and the excessive doubt and anxiety in the gentleman's appearance. My smile, which, Heaven knows, meant no encouragement, decided him; timidity instantly gave way to joy; he entered. What was to be done? I could not turn him out again; I was not answerable for any foolish conclusions he might draw, from what he ought in politeness to have considered as a thing of course. All I could do was to blame Josephine for being a French woman. To defend her, and flatter me, was the gentleman's part; and, for an Englishman, he really acquitted himself with tolerable grace. Josephine at least was pleased, and she found such a perpetual employment for monsieur, and his advice was so necessary, that there was no chance of his departure: so we talked of French toilettes, &c. &c. in French, for Josephine's edification: L— paid me some compliments upon the recovery of my looks after my illness—I thought I looked terribly languid—but he assured me that this languor, in his eyes, was an additional grace; I could not understand this: he fancied that must be because he did not express himself well in French; he explained himself more clearly in English, which Josephine, you know, does not understand, so that she was now forced to be silent, and I was compelled to take my share in the conversation. L— made me comprehend, that languor, indicating sensibility of heart, was to him the most touching of female charms; I sighed, and took up the book I had been reading; it was the new novel which you sent me, dear Gabrielle; I talked of it, in hopes of changing the course of the conversation; alas! this led to one far more dangerous: he looked at the passage I had been reading. This brought us back to sensibility again—to sentiments and descriptions so terribly apposite! we found such a similarity in our tastes! Yet L— spoke only in general, and he preserved a command over himself, which provoked me, though I knew it to be coquetry; I saw the struggle in his mind, and was determined to force him to be candid, and to enjoy my triumph. With these views I went farther than I had intended. The charm of sensibility he had told me was to him irresistible. Alas! I let him perceive all the weakness of my heart.—Sensibility is the worst time-keeper in the world. We were neither of us aware of its progressive motion. The Swiss—my evil genius—the Swiss knocked at the door to let me know dinner was served. Dinner! on what vulgar incidents the happiness of life depends! Dinner came between the discovery of my sentiments and that declaration of passion which I now must hear—or die.

"Le diner! mon Dieu!" cried Josephine. "Mais—finissons donc—la toilette de madame."

I heard the impertinent Swiss at the other end of the gallery at his master's door, wondering in broken English where his master could be, and conjecturing forty absurdities about his boots, and his being out riding, &c. &c. To sally forth in conscious innocence upon the enemy's spies, and to terminate the adventure as it was begun, à la Francoise, was my resolution. L— and Josephine understood me perfectly.

"Eh! Monsieur de Vaud," said Josephine to the Swiss, whom we met on the landing-place of the stairs, "madame n'est elle pas coeffée à ravir aujourd'hui? C'est que monsieur vient d'assister à la toilette de madame." The Swiss bowed, and said nothing. The bow was to his master, not to me, and it was a bow of duty, not of inclination. I never saw a man look so like a machine; he did not even raise his eyes upon me or my coiffure as we passed.

"Bah!" cried Josephine, with an inexpressible accent of mingled indignation and contempt. She ran down stairs, leaving the Swiss to his stupidity. I was more afraid of his penetration. But I entered the dining-room as if nothing extraordinary had happened; and after all, you know, my dear Gabrielle, nothing extraordinary had befallen us. A gentleman had assisted at a lady's toilette. Nothing more simple, nothing, more proper in the meridian of Paris; and does propriety change with meridians? There was company at dinner, and the conversation was general and uninteresting; L— endeavoured to support his part with vivacity; but he had fits of absence and silence, which might have alarmed Leonora, if she had any suspicion. But she is now perfectly secure, and absolutely blind: therefore you see there can be no danger for her happiness in my remaining where I am. For no earthly consideration would I disturb her peace of mind; there is no sacrifice I would hesitate for a moment to make to friendship or virtue, but I cannot surely be called upon to plant a dagger in my own heart to destroy, for ever to destroy my own felicity without advantage to my friend. My attachment to L—, as you say, is involuntary, and my love as pure as it is fervent. I have reason to believe that his sentiments are the same for me; but of this I am not yet certain. There is the danger, and the only real danger for Leonora's happiness; for whilst this uncertainty and his consequent fits of absence and imprudence last, there is hazard every moment of her being alarmed. But when L— once decides, every thing arranges itself, you know, Gabrielle, and prudence becomes a duty to ourselves and to Leonora. No word, or look, or coquetry could then escape us; we should be unpardonable if we did not conduct ourselves with the most scrupulous delicacy and attention to her feelings. I am amazed that L—, who has really a good understanding, does not make these reflections, and is not determined by this calculation. For his, for my own, but most for Leonora's sake, I wish that this cruel suspense were at an end. Adieu, dear and amiable Gabrielle.—These things are managed better in France.

OLIVIA.

LETTER XL

MRS. C— TO MISS B—.

DEAR MARGARET, L— Castle.

I arrived here late yesterday evening in high spirits, and high hopes of surprising and delighting all the world by my unexpected appearance; but my pride was checked, and my tone changed the moment I saw Leonora. Never was any human being so altered in her looks in so short a time. I had just, and but just presence of mind enough not to say so. I am astonished that it does not strike Mr. L—. As soon as she left the room, I asked him if Lady Leonora had been ill? No; perfectly well! perfectly well!—Did not he perceive that she looked extremely ill? No; she might be paler than usual: that was all that Mr. L— had observed. Lady Olivia, after a pause, added, that Leonora certainly had not appeared well lately, but this was nothing extraordinary in her situation. Situation! nonsense! Lady Olivia went on with sentimental hypocrisy of look and tone, saying fine things, to which I paid little attention. Virtue in words, and vice in actions! thought I. People, of certain pretensions in the court of sentiment, think that they can pass false virtues upon the world for real, as some ladies, entitled by their rank to wear jewels, appear in false stones, believing that it will be taken for granted they would wear nothing but diamonds. Not one eye in a hundred detects the difference at first, but in time the hundredth eye comes, and then they must for ever hide their diminished rays. Beware! Lady Olivia, beware!

Leonora is ill, or unhappy, or both; but she will not allow that she is either. On one subject she is impenetrable: a hundred, a thousand different ways within these four-and-twenty hours have I led to it, with all the ingenuity and all the delicacy of which I am mistress; but all to no purpose. Neither by provocation, persuasion, laughing, teazing, questioning, cross, or round about, pushing, squeezing, encompassing, taking for granted, wondering, or blundering, could I gain my point. Every look guarded— every syllable measured—yet unequivocal—

"She said no more than just the thing she ought."

Because I could find no fault, I was half angry. I respect the motive of this reserve; but towards me it is misplaced, and ill-judged, and it must not exist. I have often declared that I would never condescend to play the part of a confidante to any princess or heroine upon earth. But Leonora is neither princess nor heroine, and I would be her confidante, but she will not let me. Now I am punished for my pride. If she would only trust me, if she would only tell me what has passed since I went, and all that now weighs upon her mind, I could certainly be of some use. I could and would say every thing that she might scruple to hint to Lady Olivia, and I will answer for it I would make her raise the siege. But I cannot believe Mr. L— to be such a madman as to think of attaching himself seriously to a woman like Olivia, when he has such a wife as Leonora. That he was amusing himself with Olivia I saw, or thought I saw, some time ago, and I rather wondered that Leonora was uneasy: for all husbands will flirt, and all wives must bear it, thought I. When such a coquette as this fell in his way, and made advances, he would have been more than man if he had receded. Of course, I thought, he must despise and laugh at her all the time he was flattering and gallanting her ladyship. This would have been fair play, and comic; but the comedy should have ended by this time. I am now really afraid it will turn into a tragedy. I, even I! am alarmed. I must prevail upon Leonora to speak to me without reserve. I see her suffer, and I must share her grief. Have not I always done so from the time we were children? and now, when she most wants a friend, am not I worthy to share her confidence? Can she mistake friendship for impertinent curiosity? Does not she know that I would not be burthened with the secrets of any body whom I did not love? If she thinks otherwise, she does me injustice, and I will tell her so before I sleep. She does not know how well I love her.

My dear Margaret, Leonora and I have had a quarrel—the first serious quarrel we ever had in our lives; and the end of it is, that she is an angel, and I am a fool. Just as I laid down my pen after writing to you, though it was long past midnight, I marched into Leonora's apartment, resolved to surprise or to force her confidence. I found her awake, as I expected, and up and dressed, as I did not expect, sitting in her dressing-room, her head leaning upon her hand. I knew what she was thinking of; she had a heap of Mr. L—'s old letters beside her. She denied that she was in tears, and I will not swear to the tears, but I think

I saw signs of them notwithstanding. I spoke out;—but in vain—all in vain. At last I flew into a passion, and reproached her bitterly. She answered me with that air of dignified tenderness which is peculiar to her—"If you believe me to be unhappy, my dear Helen, is this a time to reproach me unjustly?" I was brought to reason and to tears, and after asking pardon, like a foolish naughty child, was kissed and forgiven, upon a promise never to do so any more; a promise which I hope Heaven will grant me grace and strength of mind enough to keep. I was certainly wrong to attempt to force her secret from her. Leonora's confidence is always given, never yielded; and in her, openness is a virtue, not a weakness. But I wish she would not contrive to be always in the right. In all our quarrels, in all the variations of my humour, I am obliged to end by doing homage to her reason, as the Chinese mariners, in every change of weather, burn incense before the needle.

Your affectionate

HELEN C—.

MR. L— TO GENERAL B—.

MY DEAR GENERAL, L— Castle, Friday.

I hoped that you would have favoured us with a passing visit in your way from town, but I know you will tell me that friendship must not interfere with the interests of the service. I have reason to curse those interests; they are for ever at variance with mine. I had a particular desire to speak to you upon a subject, on which it is not agreeable to me to write. Lady Leonora also wished extremely, and disinterestedly, for your company. She does not know how much she is obliged to you. The laconic advice you gave me, some time ago, influenced my conduct longer, than counsel which is in opposition to our passions usually does, and it has haunted my imagination perpetually:—"My dear L—, do not end by being the dupe of a Frenchified coquette."

My dear friend, of that there is no danger. No man upon earth despises or detests coquettes more than I do, be they French or English. I think, however, that a foreign-born, or foreign-bred coquette, has more of the ease of practice, and less of the awkwardness of conscience, than a home-bred flirt, and is in reality less blamable, for she breaks no restraints of custom or education; she does only what she has seen her mother do before her, and what is authorized by the example of most of the fashionable ladies of her acquaintance. But let us put flirts and coquettes quite out of the question. My dear general, you know that I am used to women, and take it upon my word, that the lady to whom I allude is more tender and passionate than vain. Every woman has, or has had, a tincture of vanity; but there are a few, and those are to me the most amiable of the sex, who

"Feel every vanity in fondness lost."

You know that I am delicate, even fastidious, in my taste for female manners. Nothing can in my opinion make amends for any offence against propriety, except it be sensibility—genuine, generous sensibility. This can, in my mind, cover a multitude of faults. There is so much of selfishness, of hypocrisy, of coldness, in what is visually called female virtue, that I often turn with distaste from those to whom I am compelled to do homage, for the sake of the general good of society. I am not charlatan enough to pretend upon all occasions to prefer the public advantage to my own. I confess, that let a woman be ever so fair, or good, or wise:

"Be she with that goodness blest
Which may merit name of best,
If she be not such to me,
What care I how good she be?"

And I will further acknowledge, that I am not easily satisfied with the manner in which a woman is kind to me: if it be duty-work kindness, I would not give thanks for it: it is done for her reputation, not for me, and let the world thank her. To the best of wives, I should make the worst of husbands. No—I should, I hope, pay her in her own coin, with all due observances, attentions, and respect, but without one grain of love. Love is only to be had for love; and without it, nothing a woman can give appears to me worth having. I do not desire to be loved well enough to satisfy fathers and mothers, and uncles and aunts; well enough to decide a woman to marry me rather than disoblige her friends, or run the chance of having many a worse offer, and living perhaps to be an old maid. I do not desire to be loved well enough to keep a woman true and faithful to me "till death us do part:" in short, I do not desire to be loved well enough for a husband; I desire to be loved sufficiently for a lover; not only above all other persons, but above all other things, all other considerations—to be the first and last object in the heart of the woman to whom I am attached: I wish to feel that I sustain and fill the whole of her heart. I must be certain that I am every thing to her, as she is every thing to me; that there is no imaginable situation in which she would not live with me, in which she would not be happy to live with me; no possible sacrifice that she would not make for me; or rather, that nothing she could do should appear a sacrifice. Are these exorbitant expectations? I am capable of all this, and more, for a woman I love; and it is my pride or my misfortune to be able to love upon no other terms. Such proofs of attachment it may be difficult to obtain, and even to give; more difficult, I am sensible, for a wife than for a mistress. A young lady who is married secundum artem, with licence and consent of friends, can give no extraordinary instances of affection. I should not consider it as an indisputable proof of love, that she does me the honour to give me her hand in a church, or that she condescends to bespeak my liveries, or to be handed into her own coach with all the blushing honours of a bride; all the paraphernalia of a wife secured, all the prudent and necessary provision made both for matrimonial love and hatred, dower, pin-money, and separate maintenance on the one hand, and on the other, lands, tenements, and hereditaments for the future son and heir, and sums without end for younger children to the tenth and twentieth possibility, as the case may be, nothing herein contained to the contrary in any wise notwithstanding. Such a jargon Cupid does not understand. A woman may love this most convenient personage, her lawful husband; but I should think it difficult for the delicacy of female passion to survive the cool preparations for hymeneal felicity. At all events, you will allow the lady makes no sacrifice, she shows no great generosity, and she may, or she may not, be touched at the altar by the divine flame. My good general, when you are a husband you will feel these things as I do; till then, it is very easy to talk as you do, and to admire other men's wives, and to wish Heaven had blessed you with such a treasure. For my part, the single idea, that a woman thinks it her duty to be fond of me, would deprive me of all pleasure in her love. No man can be more sensible than I am of the amiable and estimable qualities of Lady Leonora L—; I should be a brute and a liar if I hesitated to give the fullest testimony in her praise; but such is the infirmity of my nature, that I could pardon some faults more easily, than I could like some virtues. The virtues which leave me in doubt of a woman's love, I can esteem, but that is all. Lady Leonora is calm, serene, perfectly sweet-tempered, without jealousy and without suspicion; in one word, without love. If she loved me, she never could have been the wife she has been for some months past. You will laugh at my being angry with a wife for not being jealous. But so it is. Certain defects of temper I could bear, if I considered them as symptoms of strong affection. When I for a moment believed that Leonora suffered, when I attributed her fainting at our fête champêtre to jealousy, I was so much alarmed and touched, that I absolutely forgot her rival. I did more; to prevent her feeling uneasiness, to destroy the suspicions which I imagined had been awakened in her mind, I hesitated not to sacrifice all the pleasure and all the vanity which a man of my age might reasonably be supposed to feel in the prospect of a new and not inglorious conquest; I left home immediately, and went to meet you, my dear friend, on your return from abroad. This visit I do not set down to your account, but to that of honour—foolish, unnecessary honour. You half-persuaded me, that your hearsay Parisian evidence was more to be trusted than my own judgment, and I returned home with the resolution not to be the dupe of a coquette. Leonora's reception of me was delightful; I never saw her in such spirits, or so amiable. But I could not help wishing to ascertain whether I had attributed her fainting to the real cause. This proof I tempted to my cost. Instead of showing any tender alarm at the renewal of my obvious attentions to her rival, she was perfectly calm and collected, went on with her usual occupations, fulfilled all her duties, never reproached me by word or look, never for one moment betrayed impatience, ill-humour, suspicion, or jealousy; in short, I found that I had been fool enough to attribute to excess of affection, an accident which proceeded merely from the situation of her health. If anxiety of mind had been the cause of her fainting at the fête champêtre, she would since have felt and shown agitation on a thousand occasions, where she has been perfectly tranquil. Her friend Mrs. C—, who returned here a few days ago, seems to imagine that Leonora looks ill; but I shall not again be led to mistake bodily indisposition for mental suffering. Leonora's conduct argues great insensibility of soul, or great command; great insensibility, I think: for I cannot imagine such command of temper possible to any, but a woman who feels indifference for the offender. Yet, even now that I have steeled myself with this conviction, I am scarcely bold enough to hazard the chance of giving her pain. Absurd weakness! It has been clearly proved to my understanding, that my irresolution, my scruples of conscience, my combats between love and esteem, are more likely to betray the real state of my mind than any decision that I could make. I decide, then—I determine to be happy with a woman who has a soul capable of feeling, not merely what is called conjugal affection, but the passion of love; who is capable of sacrificing every thing to love; who has given me proofs of candour and greatness of mind, which I value far above all her wit, grace, and beauty. My dear general, I know all that you can tell, all that you can hint concerning her history abroad. I know it from her own lips. It was told to me in a manner that made her my admiration. It was told to me as a preservative against the danger of loving her. It was told to me with the generous design of protecting Leonora's happiness; and all this at the moment when I was beloved, tenderly beloved. She is above dissimulation: she scorns the arts, the fears of her sex. She knows you are her enemy, and yet she esteems you; she urged me to speak to you with the utmost openness: "Let me never," said she, "be the cause of your feeling less confidence or less affection for the best of friends."

R— is sacrificed to me; that R—, with whose cursed name you tormented me. My dear friend, she will force your admiration, as she has won my love.

Yours sincerely,

F. L—.

MRS. C— TO MISS B—.

L— Castle.

As I am not trusted with the secret, I may, my dear Margaret, use my own eyes and ears as I please to find it out; and I know Leonora's countance so well, that I see every thing that passes in her mind, just as clearly as if she had told it to me in words.

It grieves me, more than I can express, to see her suffering as she does. I am now convinced that she has reason to be unhappy; and what is worse, I do not see what course she can follow to recover her happiness. All her forbearance, all her patience, all her sweet temper, I perceive, are useless, or worse than useless, injurious to her in her strange husband's opinion. I never liked him thoroughly, and now I detest him. He thinks her cold, insensible! She insensible!—Brute! Idiot! Every thing that she says or does displeases him. The merest trifles excite the most cruel suspicions. He totally misunderstands her character, and sees every thing about her in a false light. In short, he is under the dominion of an artful fiend, who works as she pleases upon his passions—upon his pride, which is his ruling passion.

This evening Lady Olivia began confessing that she had too much sensibility, that she was of an excessively susceptible temper, and that she should be terribly jealous of the affections of any person she loved. She did not know how love could exist without jealousy. Mr. L— was present, and listening eagerly. Leonora's lips were silent; not so her countenance. I was in hopes Mr. L— would have remarked its beautiful touching expression; but his eyes were fixed upon Olivia. I could have ... but let me go on. Lady Olivia had the malice suddenly to appeal to Leonora, and asked whether she was never jealous of her husband? Leonora, astonished by her assurance, paused for an instant, and then replied, "It would be difficult to convince me that I had any reason to be jealous of Mr. L—, I esteem him so much."—"I wish to Heaven!" exclaimed Lady Olivia, her eyes turned upwards with a fine St. Cecilia expression, whilst Mr. L—'s attention was fixed upon her, "Would to Heaven I was blessed with such a reasonable temper!"—"When you are wishing to Heaven, Lady Olivia," said I, "had not you better ask for all you want at once; not only such a reasonable temper, but such a feeling heart?"

Some of the company smiled. Lady Olivia, practised as she is, looked disconcerted; Mr. L— grave and impenetrable; Leonora, blushing, turned away to the piano-forte. Mr. L— remained talking with Lady Olivia, and he neither saw nor heard her. If Leonora had sung like an angel, it would have made no impression. She turned over the leaves of her music quickly, to a lively air, and played it immediately, to prevent my perceiving how much she felt. Poor Leonora! you are but a bad dissembler, and it is in vain to try to conceal yourself from me.

I was so sorry for her, and so incensed with Olivia this night, that I could not restrain myself, and I made matters worse. At supper I came almost to open war with her ladyship. I cannot remember exactly what I said, but I know that I threw out the most severe inuendoes which politeness could permit: and what was the consequence? Mr. L— pitied Olivia and hated me; Leonora was in misery the whole time; and her husband probably thought that she was the instigator, though she was perfectly innocent. My dear Margaret, where will all this end? and how much more mischief shall I do with the best intentions possible?

Yours affectionately,

HELEN C—.

LETTER XLIII

GENERAL B— TO MR. L—.

Your letter has travelled after me God knows where, my dear L—, and has caught me at last with my foot in the stirrup. I have just had time to look it over. I find, in short, that you are in love. I give you joy! But be in love like a madman, not like a fool. Call a demirep an angel, and welcome; but remember, that such angels are to be had any day in the year; and such a wife as yours is not to be had for the mines of Golconda. Coin your heart, and drop your blood for it, and you will never be loved by any other woman so well as you are by Lady Leonora L—.

As to your jealous hypochondriacism, more of that when I have more leisure. In the mean time I wish it well cured.

I am, my dear friend,

Yours truly,

J. B.

LETTER XLIV

OLIVIA TO MADAME DE P—.

L— Castle.

I Triumph! dear Gabrielle, give me joy! Never was triumph more complete. L— loves me! That I knew long ago; but I have at last forced from his proud heart the avowal of his passion. Love and Olivia are victorious over scruples, prejudice, pride, and superstition!

Leonora feels not—sees not: she requires, she excites no pity. Long may her delusion last! But even were it this moment to dissipate, what cause have I for remorse? "Who is most to blame, he who ceases to love, or she who ceases to please?" Leonora perhaps thinks that she loves her husband; and no doubt she does so in a conjugal sort of a way: he has loved his wife; but be it mine to prove that his heart is suited to far other raptures; and if Olivia be called upon for sacrifices, Olivia can make them.

"Let wealth, let honour wait the wedded dame, August her deed, and sacred be her fame; Before true passion, all those views remove, Fame, wealth, and honour, what are you to love?"

These lines, though quoted perpetually by the tender and passionate, can never become stale and vulgar; they will always recur in certain situations to persons of delicate sensibility, for they at once express all that can be said, and justify all that can be felt. My amiable Gabrielle, adieu. Pardon me if to-day I have no soul even for friendship. This day is all for love.

OLIVIA.

GENERAL B— TO MR. L—.

What the devil would you have of your wife, my dear L—? You would be loved above all earthly considerations; honour, duty, virtue, and religion inclusive, would you? and you would have a wife with her head in the clouds, would you? I wish you were married to one of the all-for-love heroines, who would treat you with bowl and dagger every day of your life. In your opinion sensibility covers a multitude of faults—you would have said sins: so it had need, for it produces a multitude. Pray what brings hundreds and thousands of women to the Piazzas of Covent Garden but sensibility? What does the colonel's, and the captain's, and the ensign's mistress talk of but sensibility? And are you, my dear friend, to be duped by this hackneyed word? And should you really think it an indisputable proof of a lady's love, that she would jump out of a two pair of stairs window into your arms? Now I should think myself sure of such a woman's love only just whilst I held her, and scarcely then; for I, who in my own way am jealous as well as yourself, should in this case be jealous of wickedness, and should strongly suspect that she would love the first devil that she saw better than me.

You are always raving about sacrifices. Your Cupid must be a very vindictive little god. Mine is a good-humoured, rosy little fellow, who desires no better than to see me laugh and he happy. But to every man his own Cupid. If you cannot believe in love without sacrifices, you must have them, to be sure. And now, in sober sadness, what do you think your heroine would sacrifice for you? Her reputation? that, pardon me, is out of her power. Her virtue? I have no doubt she would. But before I can estimate the value of this sacrifice, I must know whether she makes it to you or to her pleasure. Would she give up in any instance her pleasure for your happiness? This is not an easy matter to ascertain with respect to a mistress: but your wife has put it beyond a doubt, that she prefers your happiness not only to her pleasure, but to her pride, and to every thing that the sex usually prefer to a husband. You have been wounded by a poisoned arrow; but you have a faithful wife who can extract the poison. Lady Leonora's affection is not a mere fit of goodness and generosity, such as I have seen in many women, but it is a steadiness of attachment in the hour of trial, which I have seen in few. For several months past you have, by your own account, put her temper and her love to the most severe tests, yet she has never failed for one moment, never reproached you by word or look.—But may be she has no feeling.—No feeling! you can have none, if you say so: no penetration, if you think so. Would not you think me a tyrant if I put a poor fellow on the picket, and told you, when he bore it without a groan, that it was because he could not feel? You do worse, you torture the soul of the woman who loves you; she endures, she is calm, she smiles upon you even in agony; and you tell me she cannot feel! she cannot feel like an Olivia! No; and so much the better for her husband, for she will then have only feeling enough for him, she will not extend her charity to all his sex. But Olivia has such candour and magnanimity, that I must admire her! I humbly thank her for offering to make me her confidant, for offering to tell me what I know already, and what she is certain that I know. These were good moves, but I understand the game as well as her ladyship does. As to her making a friend of me; if she means an enemy to Lady Leonora L—, I would sooner see her—in heaven: but if she would do me the favour to think no more of your heart, which is too good for her, and to accept of my—my—what shall I say?—my devoirs, I am at her command. She shall drive my curricle, &c. &c. She would suit me vastly well for a month or two, and by that time poor R— would make his appearance, or somebody in his stead: at the worst, I should have a chance of some blessed metaphysical quirk, which would prove that inconstancy was a virtue, or that a new love is better than an old one. When it came to that, I should make my best bow, put on my most disconsolate face, and retire.

You will read all this in a very different spirit from that in which it is written. If you are angry—no matter: I am cool. I tell you beforehand, that I will not fight you for any thing I have said in this letter, or that I ever may say about your Olivia. Therefore, my dear L—, save yourself the trouble of challenging me. I thank God I have reputation enough to be able to dispense with the glory of blowing out your brains.

Yours truly,

J. B.

LETTER XLVI

OLIVIA TO MADAME DE P—.

We have been very gay here the last few days: the gallant and accomplished Prince — has been here. H—, the witty H—, who is his favourite companion, introduced him; and he seems so much charmed with the old castle, its towers and battlements, and with its cynosure, that I know not when he will be able to prevail upon himself to depart. To-morrow, he says; but so he has said these ten days: he cannot resist the entreaties of his kind host and hostess to stay another day. The soft accent of the beautiful Leonora will certainly detain him one day more, and her gracious smile will bereave him of rest for months to come. He has evidently fallen desperately in love with her. Now we shall see virtue in danger.

I have always been of opinion with St. Evremond and Ninon de l'Enclos, that no female virtue can stand every species of test; fortunately it is not always exposed to trial. Reputation may be preserved by certain persons in certain situations, upon very easy terms. Leonora, for instance, is armed so strong in character, that no common mortal will venture to attack her. It would be presumption little short of high treason to imagine the fall of the Lady Leonora L—, the daughter of the Duchess of —, who, with a long line of immaculate baronesses in their own right, each in her armour of stiff stays, stands frowning defiance upon the adventurous knights. More alarming still to the modern seducer, appears a judge in his long wig, and a jury with their long faces, ready to bring in their verdict, and to award damages proportionate to the rank and fortune of the parties. Then the former reputation of the lady is talked of, and the irreparable injury sustained by the disconsolate husband from the loss of the solace and affection of this paragon of wives. And it is proved that she lived in the most perfect harmony with him, till the vile seducer appeared; who, in aggravation of damages, was a confidential friend of the husband's, &c. &c. &c. &c. &c.

Brave, indeed, and desperately in love must be the man, who could dare all these to deserve the fair. But princes are, it is said, naturally brave, and ambitious of conquering difficulties.

I have insinuated these reflections in a general way to L—, who applies them so as to plague himself sufficiently. Heaven is my witness, that I mean no injury to Lady Leonora; yet I fear that there are moments, when my respect for her superiority, joined to the consciousness of my own weakness, overpowers me, and I almost envy her the right she retains to the esteem of the man I love. This is a blamable weakness—I know it—I reproach myself bitterly; but all I can do is to confess it candidly. L— sees my conflicts, and knows how to value the sensibility of my fond heart. Adieu, my Gabrielle. When shall I be happy? since even love has its torments, and I am thus doomed to be ever a victim to the tenderness of my soul.

OLIVIA.

LETTER XLVII

MRS. C— TO MISS B—.

I do not know whether I pity, love, or admire Leonora most. Just when her mind was deeply wounded by her husband's neglect, and when her jealousy was worked to the highest pitch by his passion for her dangerous rival, the Prince — arrives here, and struck by Leonora's charms of mind and person, falls passionately in love with her. Probably his highness's friend H— had given him a hint of the existing circumstances, and he thought a more propitious moment could scarcely be found for making an impression upon a female mind. He judged of Leonora by other women. And I, like a simpleton, judged of her by myself. With shame I confess to you, my dear Margaret, that notwithstanding all my past experience, I did expect that she would have done, as I am afraid I should have done in her situation. I think that I could not have resisted the temptation of coquetting a little—a very little—just to revive the passion of the man whom I really loved. This expedient succeeds so often with that wise sex, who never rightly know the value of a heart, except when they have just won it, or at the moment when they are on the point of losing it. In Leonora's place and in such an emergency, I should certainly have employed that frightful monster jealousy to waken sleeping love; since he, and only he, can do it expeditiously and effectually. This I have hinted to Leonora, talking always in generals; for, since my total overthrow, I have never dared to come to particulars: but by putting cases and confessing myself, I contrived to make my thoughts understood. I then boasted of the extreme facility of the means I would adopt to recover a heart. Leonora answered in the words of a celebrated great man:—"C'est facile de se servir de pareils moyens; c'est difficile de s'y r'soudre."

"But if no other means would succeed," said I, "would not you sacrifice your pride to your love?"

"My pride, willingly; but not my sense of what is right," said she, with an indescribable mixture of tenderness and firmness in her manner.

"Can a little coquetry in a good cause be such a heinous offence?" persisted I. I knew that I was wrong all the time; but I delighted in seeing how right she was.

No—she would not allow her mind to be cheated by female sophistry; nor yet by the male casuistry of, "the end sanctifies the means."

"If you had the misfortune to lose the affections of the man you love, and if you were quite certain of regaining them by following my recipe?" said I.

Never shall I forget the look with which Leonora left me, and the accent with which she said, "My dear Helen, if it were ever to be my misfortune to lose my husband's love, I would not, even if I were certain of success, attempt to regain it by any unworthy arts. How could I wish to regain his love at the hazard of losing his esteem, and the certainty of forfeiting my own!"

I said no more—I had nothing more to say: I saw that I had given pain, and I have never touched upon the subject since. But her practice is even beyond her theory. Never, by deed, or look, or word, or thought (for I see all her thoughts in her eloquent countenance), has she swerved from her principles. No prudery—no coquetry—no mock-humility—no triumph. Never for an instant did she, by a proud air, say to her husband,—See what others think of me! Never did a resentful look say to him—Inconstant!— revenge is in my power! Never even did a reproachful sigh express—I am injured, yet I do not retaliate.

Mr. L—is blind; he is infatuated; he is absolutely bereaved of judgment by a perfidious, ungrateful, and cruel wretch. Let me vent my indignation to you, dear Margaret, or it will explode, perhaps, when it may do Leonora mischief. Yours affectionately, Helen C—.

LETTER XLVIII

OLIVIA TO MADAME DE F—.

L— Castle.

This Lady Leonora, in her simplicity, never dreamed of love till the prince's passion was too visible and audible to be misunderstood: and then she changed her tone, and checked her simplicity, and was so reserved, and so dignified, and so proper, it was quite edifying, especially to a poor sinner of a coquette like me; nothing piquante; nothing agaçante; nothing demi-voilée; no retiring to be pursued; not a single manoeuvre of coquetry did she practise. This convinces me that she cares not in the least for her husband; because, if she really loved him, and wished to reclaim his heart, what so natural or so simple as to excite his jealousy, and thus revive his love? After neglecting this golden opportunity, she can never convince me that she is really anxious about her husband's heart. This I hinted to L—, and his own susceptibility had hinted it to him efficaciously, before I spoke.

Though Leonora has been so correct hitherto, and so cold to the prince in her husband's presence, I have my suspicions that, if in his absence, proper means were taken, if her pride were roused by apt suggestions, if it were delicately pointed out to her that she is shamefully neglected, that she is a cipher in her own house, that her husband presumes too much upon her sweetness of temper, that his inconstancy is wondered at by all who have eyes, and that a little retaliation might become her ladyship, I would not answer for her forbearance, that is to say if all this were done by a dexterous man, a lover and a prince! I shall take care my opinions shall be known; for I cannot endure to have the esteem of the man I love monopolized. Exposed to temptation, as I have been, and with as ardent affections, Leonora, or I am much mistaken, would not have been more estimable. Adieu, my dearest Gabrielle. Nous verrons! nous verrons!

OLIVIA.

Sunday evening.

P.S. I open my letter to tell you that the prince is actually gone. Doubtless he will return at a more auspicious moment.

Lady M— and all the troop of friends are to depart on Monday; all but the bosom friend, l'amie intime, that insupportable Helen, who is ever at daggers-drawing with me. So much the better! L— sees her cabals with his wife; she is a partisan without the art to be so to any purpose, and her manoeuvres tend only to increase his partiality for his Olivia.

LETTER XLIX

OLIVIA TO MADAME DE P—.

L— Castle.

In short, Leonora has discovered all that she might have seen months ago between her husband and me. What will be the consequence? I long, yet almost fear, to meet her again. She is now in her own apartment, writing, I presume, to her mother for advice.

LETTER L

LEONORA TO OLIVIA.

[Left on Lady Olivia's dressing-table.]

O you, whom no kindness can touch, whom no honour can bind, whom no faith can hold, enjoy the torments you have inflicted on me! enjoy the triumph of having betrayed a confiding friend! Friend no more—affect, presume no longer to call me friend! I am under no necessity to dissemble, and dissimulation is foreign to my habits, and abhorrent to my nature! I know you to be my enemy, and I say so—my most cruel enemy; one who could, without reluctance or temptation, rob me of all I hold most dear. Yes, without temptation; for you do not love my husband, Olivia. On this point I cannot be mistaken; I know too well what it is to love him. Had you been struck by his great or good and amiable qualities, charmed by his engaging manners, or seduced by the violence of his passion; and had I seen you honourably endeavour to repress that passion; had I seen in you the slightest disposition to sacrifice your pleasure or your vanity to friendship or to duty, I think I could have forgiven, I am sure I should have pitied you. But you felt no pity for me, no shame for yourself; you made no attempt to avoid, you invited the danger. Mr. L— was not the deceiver, but the deceived. By every art and every charm in your power—and you have many—you won upon his senses and worked upon his imagination; you saw, and made it your pride to conquer the scruples of that affection he once felt for his wife, and that wife was your friend. By passing bounds, which he could not conceive that any woman could pass, except in the delirium of passion, you made him believe that your love for him exceeds all that I feel. How he will find himself deceived! If you had loved him as I do, you could not so easily have forfeited all claim to his esteem. Had you loved him so much, you would have loved honour more.

It is possible that Mr. L— may taste some pleasure with you whilst his delusion lasts, whilst his imagination paints you, as mine once did, in false colours, possessed of generous virtues, and the victim of excessive sensibility: but when he sees you such as you are, he will recoil from you with aversion, he will reject you with contempt.

Knowing my opinion of you, Lady Olivia, you will not choose to remain in this house; nor can I desire for my guest one whom I can no longer, in private or in public, make my companion.

Adieu.

Leonora L—.

LETTER LI

OLIVIA TO MR. L—.

L— Castle, Midnight.

Farewell for ever!—It must be so—Farewell for ever! Would to Heaven I had summoned courage sooner to pronounce these fatal, necessary, irrevocable words: then had I parted from you without remorse, without the obloquy to which I am now exposed. Oh, my dearest L—! Mine, do I still dare to call you? Yes, mine for the last time, I must call you, mine I must fancy you, though for the impious thought the Furies themselves were to haunt me to madness. My dearest L—, never more must we meet in this world! Think not that my weak voice alone forbids it: no, a stronger voice than mine is heard—an injured wife reclaims you. What a letter have I just received...!—from.....Leonora! She tells me that she no longer desires for her guest one whom she cannot, in public or private, make her companion—Oh, Leonora, it was sufficient to banish me from your heart! She tells me not only that I have for ever forfeited her confidence; her esteem, her affection; but that I shall soon be your aversion and contempt. Oh, cruel, cruel words! But I submit—I have deserved it all—I have robbed her of a heart above all price. Leonora, why did you not reproach me more bitterly? I desire, I implore to be crushed, to be annihilated by your vengeance! Most admirable, most virtuous, most estimable of women, best of wives, I have with sacrilegious love profaned a soul consecrated to you and conjugal virtue. I acknowledge my crime; trample upon me as you will, I am humbled in the dust. More than all your bitterest reproaches, do I feel the remorse of having, for a moment, interrupted such serenity of happiness.

Oh, why did you persuade me, L—, and why did I believe that Leonora was calm and free from all suspicion? How could I believe that any woman whom you had ever loved, could remain blind to your inconstancy, or feel secure indifference? Happy woman! in you to love is not a crime; you may glory in your passion, whilst I must hide mine from every human eye, drop in shameful secrecy the burning tear, stifle the struggling sigh, blush at the conflicts of virtue and sensibility, and carry shame and remorse with me to the grave. Happy Leonora! happy even when most injured, you have a right to complain to him you love;—he is yours—you are his wife—his esteem, his affection are yours. On Olivia he has bestowed but a transient thought, and eternal ignominy must be her portion. So let it be—so I wish it to be. Would to Heaven I may thus atone for the past, and secure your future felicity! Fly to her, my dearest L—, I conjure you! throw yourself at her feet, entreat, implore, obtain her forgiveness. She cannot refuse it to your tears, to your caresses. To withstand them she must be more or less than woman. No, she cannot resist your voice when it speaks words of peace and love; she will press you with transport to her heart, and Olivia, poor Olivia, will be for ever forgotten; yet she will rejoice in your felicity; absolved perhaps in the eye of Heaven, though banished from your society, she will die content.

Full well am I aware of the consequences of quitting thus precipitately the house of Lady Leonora L—; but nothing that concerns myself alone can, for a moment, make me hesitate to do that, which the sentiment of virtue dictates, and which is yet more strongly urged by regard for the happiness of one, who once allowed me to call her friend. I know my reputation is irrecoverably sacrificed; but it is to one for whom I would lay down my life. Can a woman who feels as I do deem any earthly good a sacrifice for him she loves? Dear L—, adieu for ever!

Olivia.

LETTER LII

LEONORA TO THE DUCHESS OF —.

Dearest Mother,

It is all over—my husband is gone—gone perhaps for ever—all is in vain—all is lost!

Without saying more to you than I ought, I may tell you, that in consequence of an indignant letter which I wrote last night to Lady Olivia, she left my house this morning early, before any of the family were up. Mr. L— heard of her departure before I did. He has, I will not say followed her, for of that I am not certain; but he has quitted home, and without giving me one kind look at parting, without even noticing a letter which I left last night upon his table. At what slight things we catch to save us from despair! How obstinate, how vain is hope! I fondly hoped, even to the last moment, that this letter, this foolish letter, would work a sudden change in my husband's heart, would operate miracles, would restore me to happiness. I fancied, absurdly fancied, that laying open my whole soul to him would have an effect upon his mind. Alas! has not my whole soul been always open to him? Could this letter tell him any thing but what he knows already, or what he will never know—how well I love him! I was weak to expect so much from it; yet as it expressed without complaint the anguish of disappointed affection, it deserved at least some acknowledgment. Could not he have said, "My dear Leonora, I thank you for your letter?"—or more colder still—"Leonora, I have received your letter?" Even that would have been some relief to me: but now all is despair. I saw him just when he was going away, but for a moment; till the last instant he was not to be seen; then, in spite of all his command of countenance, I discerned strong marks of agitation; but towards me an air of resentment, more than any disposition to kinder thoughts. I fancy that he scarcely knew what he said, nor, I am sure, did I. He talked, I remember, of having immediate business in town, and I endeavoured to believe him. Contrary to his usual composed manner, he was in such haste to be gone, that I was obliged to send his watch and purse after him, which he had left on his dressing-table. How melancholy his room looked to me! His clothes just as he had left them—a rose which Lady Olivia gave him yesterday was in water on his table. My letter was not there; so he has it, probably unread. He will read it some time or other, perhaps—and some time or other, perhaps, when I am dead and gone, he will believe I loved him. Could he have known what I felt at the moment when he turned from me, he would have pitied me; for his nature, his character, cannot be quite altered in a few months, though he has ceased to love Leonora. From the window of his own room I watched for the last glimpse of him—heard him call to the postilions, and bid them "drive fast—faster." This was the last sound I heard of his voice. When shall I hear that voice again? I think that I shall certainly hear from him the day after to-morrow—and I wish to-day and to-morrow were gone.

I am afraid that you will think me very weak; but, my dear mother, I have no motive for fortitude now; and perhaps it might have been better for me, if I had not exerted so much. I begin to fear that all my fortitude is mistaken for indifference. Something Mr. L— said the other day, about sensibility and sacrifices, gave me this idea. Sensibility!—It has been my hard task for some months past to repress mine, that it might not give pain or disgust. I have done all that my reason and my dearest mother counselled; surely I cannot have done wrong. How apt we are to mistake the opinion or the taste of the man we love for the rule of right! Sacrifices! What sacrifices can I make?—All that I have, is it not his?—My whole heart, is it not his? Myself, all that I am, all that I can be? Have I not lived with him of late, without recalling to his mind the idea that I suffer by his neglect? Have I not left his heart at liberty, and can I make a greater sacrifice? I really do not understand what he means by sacrifices. A woman who loves her husband is part of him; whatever she does for him is for herself. I wish he would explain to me what he can mean by sacrifices—but when will he ever again explain his thoughts and feelings to me?

My dearest mother, it has been a relief to my mind to write all this to you; if there is no sense in it, you will forgive and encourage me by your affection and strength of mind, which, in all situations, have such power to soothe and support your daughter.

The prince —, who spent a fortnight here, paid me particular attention.

The prince talked of soon paying us another visit. If he should, I will not receive him in Mr. L—'s absence. This may seem like vanity or prudery; but no matter what it appears, if it be right.

Well might you, my best friend, bid me beware of forming an intimacy with an unprincipled woman. I have suffered severely for neglecting your counsels; how much I have still to endure is yet to be tried: but I can never be entirely miserable whilst I possess, and whilst I hope that I deserve, the affection of such a mother.

LEONORA L—.

LETTER LIII

THE DUCHESS OF — TO HER DAUGHTER.

If my approbation and affection can sustain you in this trying situation, your fortitude will not forsake you, my beloved daughter. Great minds rise in adversity; they are always equal to the trial, and superior to injustice: betrayed and deserted, they feel their own force, and they rely upon themselves. Be yourself, my Leonora! Persevere as you have begun, and, trust me, you will be happy. I abide by my first opinion, I repeat my prophecy—your husband's esteem, affection, love, will be permanently yours. Change of circumstances, however alarming, cannot shake the fixed judgment of my understanding.

Character, as you justly observe, cannot utterly change in a few months. Your husband is deceived, he is now as one in the delirium of a fever: he will recover his senses, and see Lady Olivia and you such as you are.

You do not explain, and I take it for granted you have good reasons for not explaining to me more fully, the immediate cause of your letter to Lady Olivia. I am sorry that any cause should have thrown her upon the protection of Mr. L—; for a man of honour and generosity feels himself bound to treat with tenderness a woman who appears to sacrifice every thing for his sake. Consider this in another point of view, and it will afford you subject of consolation; for it is always a consolation to good minds, to think those whom they love less to blame than they appear to be. You will be more calm and patient when you reflect that your husband's absence may be prolonged by a mistaken sense of honour. From the nature of his connexion with Lady Olivia it cannot last long. Had she saved appearances, and engaged him in a sentimental affair, it might have been far more dangerous to your happiness.

I entirely approve of your conduct with respect to the prince: it is worthy of my child, and just what I should have expected from her. The artifices of coquettes, and all the art of love is beneath her; she has far other powers and resources, and need not strive to maintain her dignity by vengeance. I admire your magnanimity, and I still more admire your good sense; for high spirit is more common in our sex than good sense. Few know how, and when, they should sacrifice small considerations to great ones. You say that you will not receive the prince in your husband's absence, though this may be attributed to prudery or vanity, &c. &c. You are quite right. How many silly women sacrifice the happiness of their lives to the idea of what women or men, as silly as themselves, will say or think of their motives. How many absurd heroines of romance, and of those who imitate them in real life, do we see, who can never act with common sense or presence of mind: if a man's carriage breaks down, or his horse is tired at the end of their avenues, or for some such ridiculous reason, they must do the very reverse of all they know to be prudent. Perpetually exposed, by a fatal concurrence of circumstances, to excite the jealousy of their lovers and husbands, they create the necessity to which they fall a victim. I rejoice that I cannot feel any apprehension of my daughter's conducting herself like one of these novel-bred ladies.

I am sorry, my dear, that Lady M— and your friends have left you: yet even in this there may he good. Your affairs will be made less public, and you will be less the subject of impertinent curiosity. I advise you, however, to mix as much as usual with your neighbours in the country: your presence, and the dignity of your manners, will impose silence upon idle tongues. No wife of real spirit solicits the world for compassion: she who does not court popularity ensures respect.

Adieu, my dearest child: the time will come when your husband will feel the full merit of your fortitude; when he will know how to distinguish between true and false sensibility; between the love of an Olivia and of a Leonora.

—.

LETTER LIV

MRS. C— TO MISS B—.

Jan. 26.

My Dear Margaret,

I shall never forgive myself. I fear I have done Leonora irreparable injury; and, dear magnanimous sufferer, she has never reproached me! In a fit of indignation and imprudent zeal I made a discovery, which has produced a total breach between Leonora and Lady Olivia, and in consequence of this Mr. L— has gone off with her ladyship.

We have heard nothing from Mr. L— since his departure, and Leonora is more unhappy than ever, and my imprudence is the cause of this. Yet she continues to love me. She is an angel! I have promised her not to mention her affairs in future even in any of my letters to you, dear Margaret. Pray quiet any reports you may hear, and stop idle tongues.

Yours affectionately,

Helen C—.

LETTER LV

MR. L— TO GENERAL B—.

Richmond.

My Dear Friend,

I do not think I could have borne with temper, from any other man breathing, the last letter which I received from you. I am sensible that it was written with the best intentions for my happiness; but I must now inform you, that the lady in question has accepted of my protection, and consequently no man who esteems me can treat her with disrespect.

It is no longer a question, what she will sacrifice for me; she has shown the greatest generosity and tenderness of soul; and I should despise myself, if I did not exert every power to make her happy.—We are at Richmond; but if you write, direct to me at my house in town.

Yours sincerely,

F. L—.

LETTER LVI

GENERAL B— TO MR. L—.

Dream your dream out, my dear L—. Since you are angry with me, as Solander was with Sir Joseph Banks for awakening him, I shall not take the liberty of shaking you any more. I believe I shook you rather too roughly: but I assure you it was for your good, as people always tell their friends when they do the most disagreeable things imaginable. Forgive me, and I will let you dream in peace. You will, however, allow me to watch by you, whilst you sleep; and, my dear somnambulist, I may just take care that you do not knock your head against a post, or fall into a well.

I hope you will not have any objection to my paying my respects to Lady Olivia when I come to town, which, I flatter myself, I shall be able to do shortly. The fortifications here are almost completed.

Yours truly,

J. B.

OLIVIA TO MADAME DE P—.

Richmond, —.

Happy!—No, my dear Gabrielle, nor shall I ever be happy, whilst I have not exclusive possession of the heart of the man I love. I have sacrificed every thing to him; I have a right to expect that he should sacrifice at least a wife for me—a wife whom he only esteems. But L— has not sufficient strength of mind to liberate himself from the cobwebs which restrain those who talk of conscience, and who, in fact, are only superstitious. I see with indignation, that his soul is continually struggling between passion for me and a something, I know not what to call it, that he feels for this wife. His thoughts are turning towards home. I believe that to an Englishman's ears, there is some magic in the words home and wife. I used to think foreigners ridiculous for associating the ideas of Milord Anglois with roast beef and pudding; but I begin to see that they are quite right, and that an Englishman has a certain set of inveterate homely prejudices, which are necessary to his well-being, and almost to his existence. You may entice him into the land of sentiment, and for a time keep him there; but refine and polish and enlighten him, as you will, he recurs to his own plain sense, as he terms it, on the first convenient opportunity. In short, it is lost labour to civilize him, for sooner or later he will hottentot again. Pray introduce that term, Gabrielle—you can translate it. For my part, I can introduce nothing here; my manière d'être is really insupportable; my talents are lost; I, who am accustomed to shine in society, see nobody; I might, as Josephine every day observes, as well be buried alive. Retirement and love are charming; but then it must be perfect love—not the equivocating sort that L— feels for me, which keeps the word of promise only to the ear. I bear every sort of désagrément for him; I make myself a figure for the finger of scorn to point at, and he insults me with esteem for a wife. Can you conceive this, my amiable Gabrielle?—No, there are ridiculous points in the characters of my countrymen which you will never be able to comprehend. And what is still more incomprehensible, it is my fate to love this man; yes, passionately to love him!—But he must give me proof of reciprocal passion. I have too much spirit to sacrifice every thing for him, who will sacrifice nothing for me. Besides, I have another motive. To you, my faithful Gabrielle, I open my whole heart.—Pride inspires me as well as love. I am resolved that Leonora, the haughty Leonora, shall live to repent of having insulted and exasperated Olivia. In some situations contempt can be answered only by vengeance; and when the malice of a contracted and illiberal mind provokes it, revenge is virtue. Leonora has called me her enemy, and consequently has made me such. 'Tis she has declared the war! 'tis for me to decide the victory!

L—, I know, has the offer of an embassy to Petersburg.—He shall accept it.—I will accompany him thither. Lady Leonora may, in his absence, console herself with her august counsellor and mother:—that proudest of earthly paragons is yet to be taught the extent of Olivia's power. Adieu, my charming Gabrielle! I will carry your tenderest remembrances to our brilliant Russian princess. She has often invited me, you know, to pay her a visit, and this will be the ostensible object of my journey. A horrible journey, to be sure!!!—But what will not love undertake and accomplish, especially when goaded by pride, and inspirited by great revenge?

OLIVIA.

LETTER LVIII

OLIVIA TO MR. L—.

Victim to the delusions of passion, too well I know my danger, and now, even now, foresee my miserable fate. Too well I know, that the delicious poison which spreads through my frame exalts, entrances, but to destroy. Too well I know that the meteor fire, which shines so bright on my path, entices me forward but to plunge me in the depths of infamy. The long warnings of recorded time teach me, that perjured man triumphs, disdains, and abandons. Too well, alas! I know these fatal truths; too well I feel my approaching doom. Yet, infatuated as I am, prescience avails not; the voice of prudence warns, the hand of Heaven beckons me in vain.

My friend! my more than friend, my lover! beloved beyond expression! you to whom I immolate myself, you for whom I sacrifice more than life. Oh, whisper words of peace! for you, and you alone, can tranquillize this agitated bosom. Assure me, L—, if with truth you can assure me, that I have no rival in your affections. Oh, tell me that the name of wife does not invalidate the claims of love! Repeat for me, a thousand times repeat, that I am sole possessor of your heart!

The moment you quit me I am overpowered with melancholy forebodings. Scarcely are you out of my sight, before I dread, that I shall never see you more, or that some fatality should deprive me of your love. When shall the sails of love waft us from this dangerous shore? Oh! when shall I dare to call you mine? Heavens! how many things may intervene...! Let nothing detain you from Richmond this evening; but come not at all—come no more, unless to reassure my trembling heart, and to convince me that love and Olivia have banished every other image.

Olivia.

LETTER LIX

MR. L— TO GENERAL B—.

My Dear General,

I am come to a resolution to accept of that embassy to Russia which I lately refused. My mind has been in such constant anxiety for some time past, that my health has suffered, and change of air and place are necessary to me. You will say, that the climate of Russia is a strange choice for an invalid: I could indeed have wished for a milder; but in this world we must be content with the least of two evils. I wish to have some ostensible reason for going abroad, and this embassy is the only one that presents itself in an unquestionable shape. Any thing is better than staying where I am, and as I am. My motives are not so entirely personal and selfish as I have stated them. A man who has a grain of feeling cannot endure to see the woman whom he loves, whose only failing is her love, living in a state of dereliction, exposed to the silent scorn of her equals and inferiors, if not to open insult. All her fine talents, every advantage of nature and education sacrificed, and her sensibility to shame a perpetual source of misery. A man must be a brute if he do not feel for a woman, whose affection for him has reduced her to this situation. My delicacy as to female manners, and the high value I set upon public opinion in all that concerns the sex, make me peculiarly susceptible and wretched in my present circumstances. To raise the drooping spirits, and support the self-approbation of a woman, who is conscious that she has forfeited her claim to respect—to make love supply the place of all she has sacrificed to love, is a difficult and exquisitely painful task. My feelings render hers more acute, and the very precautions which I take, however delicate, alarm and wound her pride, by reminding her of all she wishes to forget. In this country, no woman, who is not lost to shame, can bear to live without reputation.—I pass over a great many intermediate ideas, my dear general; your sense and feeling will supply them. You see the expediency, the necessity of my accepting this embassy. Olivia urges, how can I refuse it? She wishes to accompany me. She made this offer with such decision of spirit, with such passionate tenderness, as touched me to the very soul. A woman who really loves, absolutely devotes herself, and becomes insensible to every difficulty and danger; to her all parts of the world are alike; all she fears is to be separated from the object of her affections.

But the very excess of certain passions proves them to be genuine. Even whilst we blame the rashness of those who act from the enthusiasm of their natures, whilst we foresee all the perils to which they seem blind, we tremble at their danger, we grow more and more interested for them every moment, we admire their courage, we long to snatch them from their fate, we are irresistibly hurried along with them down the precipice.

But why do I say all this to you, my dear general? To no man upon earth could it be more ineffectually addressed. Let me see you, however, before we leave England. It would be painful to me to quit this country without taking leave of you, notwithstanding all that you have lately done to thwart my inclinations, and notwithstanding all I may expect you to say when we meet. Probably I shall be detained here some weeks, as I must wait for instructions from our court. I write this day to Lady Leonora, to inform her that I am appointed ambassador to Russia. She shall have all the honours of war; she shall be treated with all the respect to which she is so well entitled. I suppose she will wish to reside with her mother during my absence. She cannot do better: she will then be in the most eligible situation, and I shall be relieved from all anxiety upon her account. She will be perfectly happy with her mother. I have often thought that she was much happier before she married me, than she has been since our union.

I have some curiosity to know whether she will see the Prince when I am gone. Do not mistake me; I am not jealous: I have too little love, and too much esteem for Leonora, to feel the slightest jealousy. I have no doubt, that if I were to stay in Russia for ten years, and if all the princes and potentates in Europe were to be at her feet, my wife would conduct herself with the most edifying propriety: but I am a little curious to know how far vanity or pride can console a virtuous woman for the absence of love.

Yours truly,

F. L.

MADAME DE P— TO OLIVIA.

Paris.

You are really decided then to go to Russia, my amiable friend, and you will absolutely undertake this horrible voyage! And you are not intimidated by the idea of the immense distance between Petersburg and Paris! Alas! I had hoped soon to see you again. The journey from my convent to Paris was the longest and most formidable that I ever undertook, and at this moment it appears to me terrible; you may conceive therefore my admiration of your courage and strength of mind, my dear Olivia, who are going to brave the ocean, turning your back on Paris, and every moment receding from our polished centre of attraction, to perish perhaps among mountains of ice. Mon Dieu! it makes me shudder to think of it. But if it please Heaven that you should once arrive at Petersburg, you will crown your tresses with diamonds, you will envelope yourself with those superb furs of the north, and smiling at all the dangers you have passed, you will be yourself a thousand times more dangerous than they. You, who have lived so long at Paris, who speak our language in all its shades of elegance; you, who have divined all our secrets of pleasing, who have caught our very air,

"Et la grace, encore plus belle que la beauté;"

you, who are absolutely a French woman, and a Parisian, what a sensation you will produce at Petersburg!—Quels succès vous attendent!—Quels hommages!

You will have the goodness to offer my tenderest sentiments, and the assurances of my perfect respect, to our dear Princess; you will also find the proper moment to remind her of the promise she made, to send me specimens of the fine ermines and sables of her country. For my part, I used to be, I confess, in a great error with respect to furs: I always acknowledged them to be rich, but avoided them as heavy; I considered them as fitter for the stiff magnificence of an Empress of all the Russias than for the light elegance of a Parisian beauty; but our charming Princess convinced me that this is a heresy in taste. When I beheld the grace with which she wore her ermine, and the art with which she knew how to vary its serpent folds as she moved, or as she spoke, the variety it gave to her costume and attitudes; the development it afforded to a fine hand and arm, the resource in the pauses of conversation, and that soft and attractive air which it seemed to impart even to the play of her wit, I could no longer refuse my homage to ermine. Such is the despotism of beauty over all the objects of taste and fashion; and so it is, that a woman of sense, address, and sentiment, let her be born or thrown by fate where she may, will always know how to avail herself of every possible advantage of nature and art. Nothing will be too trifling or too vast for her genius.

I must make you understand me, my dear Olivia; your Gabrielle is not so frivolous as simpletons imagine. Frivolity is an excellent, because an unsuspected mask, under which serious and important designs may be safely concealed. I would explain myself further, but must now go to the opera to see the new ballet.

Let me know, my interesting, my sublime Olivia, when you are positively determined on your voyage to Petersburg; and then you shall become acquainted with your friend as a politician. Her friendship for you will not be confined to a mere intercourse of sentiment, but will, if you have courage to second her views, give you a secret yet decisive weight and consequence, of which you have hitherto never dreamed.—Adieu.—These gentlemen are so impatient, I must go. Burn the last page of this letter, and the whole of my next as soon as you have read it, I conjure you, my dear.

GABRIELLE DE P—.

LETTER LXI

GENERAL B— TO MR. L—.

DEAR L—,

I have time but to write one line to satisfy that philosophical curiosity, which, according to your injunctions, I will not denominate jealousy—except when I talk to myself.

You have a philosophical curiosity to know whether your wife will see the Prince in your absence. I saw his favourite yesterday, who complained to me that his highness had been absolutely refused admittance at your castle, notwithstanding he had made many ingenious, and some bold attempts, to see Lady Leonora L— in the absence of her faithless husband.

As to your scheme of going to Russia, you will be obliged, luckily, to wait for some time for instructions, and in the interval, it is to be hoped you will recover your senses. I shall see you as soon as possible.

Yours truly,

J. B.

LETTER LXII

MADAME DE P— TO LADY OLIVIA.

Paris.

As our vanity always endeavours to establish a balance between our own perfections and those of our friends, I must flatter myself, my dear Olivia, that in compensation for that courage and ardent imagination in which you are so much my superior, I possess some little advantages over you in my scientific, hereditary knowledge of court intrigue, and of the arts of representation; all which will be necessary to you in your character of ambassadress: you will in fact deserve this title, for of course you will govern the English ambassador, whom you honour with your love. And of course you will appear with splendour, and you will be particularly careful to have your traineau well appointed. Pray remember that one of your horses must gallop, whilst the other trots, or you are nobody. It will also be absolutely necessary to have a numerous retinue of servants, because this suits the Russian idea of magnificence. You must have, as the Russian nobles always had in Paris, four servants constantly to attend your equipage; one to carry the flambeau, another to open the door, and a couple to carry you into and out of your carriage. I beseech you to bear in mind perpetually, that you are to be as helpless as possible. A Frenchman of my acquaintance, who spent nine years in Russia, told me, that in his first setting out at Petersburg, he was put on his guard in this particular by a speech of his Russian valet-de-chambre:—"Sir, the Englishman you visited to-day cannot be worthy of your acquaintance; he cannot be a gentleman. Son valet me dit qu'il se déshabille seul!!!"

I suppose you take Josephine with you; she will be an inestimable treasure; and I shall make it my business to send you the first advices of Paris fashions, which her talents will not fail to comprehend and execute. My charming Olivia! you will be the model of taste and elegance! Do not suspect that dress is carrying me away from politics. I assure you I know what I am about, and am going straight to my object. The art of attending to trifles is the art of governing the world, as all historians know, who have gone to the bottom of affairs. Was not the face of Europe changed by a cup of tea thrown on Mrs. Masham's gown, as Voltaire, with penetrating genius, remarks? Women, without a doubt, understand the importance of trifles better than men do, and consequently always move in secret the slight springs of that vast machine, the civilized world. Is not your ambition roused, my Olivia? You must, however, lay aside a little of your romance, and not approach the political machine whilst you are intoxicated with love, else you will blunder infallibly, and do infinite and irreparable mischief to yourself and your friends.

Permit me to tell you, that you have been a little spoiled by sentimental novels, which are good only to talk of when one must show sensibility, but destructive as rules of action. By the false lights which these writers, who know nothing of the world, have thrown upon objects, you have been deluded; you have been led to mistake the means for the end. Love has been with you the sole end of love; whereas it ought to be the beginning of power. No matter for the past: the future is yours: at our age this future must be dexterously managed. A woman of spirit, and, what is better, of sense, must always take care that in her heart, the age of love is not prolonged beyond the age of being beloved. In these times a woman has no choice at a certain period but politics, or bel esprit; for devotion, which used to be a resource, is no longer in fashion. We must all take a part, my dear; I assure you I have taken mine decidedly, and I predict that you will take yours with brilliant success. How often must one cry in the ears of lovers—Love must die! must die! must die! But you, my dear Olivia, will not be deaf to the warning voice of common sense. Your own experience has on former occasions convinced you, that passion cannot be eternal; and at present, if I mistake not, there is in your love a certain mixture of other feelings, a certain alloy, which will make it happily ductile and manageable. When your triumph over the wife is complete, passion for the husband will insensibly decay; and this will be fortunate for you, because assuredly your ambassador would not choose to remain all the rest of his days in love and in exile at Petersburg. All these English are afflicted with the maladie du pays; and, as you observe so well, the words home and wife have ridiculous but unconquerable power over their minds. What will become of you, my friend, when this Mr. L— chooses to return to England to his castle, &c.? You could not accompany him. You must provide in time against this catastrophe, or you will be a deserted, disgraced, undone woman, my dear friend.

No one should begin to act a romance who has not well considered the denouement. It is a charming thing to mount with a friend in a balloon, amid crowds of spectators, who admire the fine spectacle, and applaud the courage of the aërostats: the losing sight of this earth, and the being in or above the clouds, must also be delightful: but the moment will come when the travellers descend, and then begins the danger; then they differ about throwing out the ballast, the balloon is rent in the quarrel, it sinks with frightful rapidity, and they run the hazard, like the poor Marquis D'Arlande, of being spitted upon the spire of the Invalides, or of being entangled among woods and briers—at last, alighting upon the earth, our adventurers, fatigued and bruised and disappointed, come out of their shattered triumphal car, exposed to the derision of the changeable multitude.

Every thing in this world is judged of by success. Your voyage to Petersburg, my dear Olivia, must not be a mere adventure of romance; as a party of pleasure it would be ridiculous; we must make something more of it. Enclosed is a letter to a Russian nobleman, an old lover of mine, who, I understand, is in favour. He will certainly be at your command. He is a man possessed by the desire of having reputation among foreigners, vain of the preference of our sex, generous even to prodigality. By his means you will be immediately placed on an easy footing with all the leading persons of the Russian court. You will go on from one step to another, till you are at the height which I have in view. Now for my grand object.—No, not now—for I have forty little notes about nothings to write this morning. Great things hang upon these nothings, so they should not be neglected. I must leave you, my amiable Olivia, and defer my grand object till to-morrow.

GABRIELLE DE P—.

LETTER LXIII

LEONORA TO THE DUCHESS OF —.

DEAR MOTHER,

This moment I have received a letter from Mr. L—. He has accepted of an embassy to Petersburg. I cannot guess by the few lines he has written, whether or not he wishes that I should accompany him. Most ardently I wish it; but if my offer should be refused, or if it should be accepted only because it could not be well refused; if I should be a burthen, a restraint upon him, I should wish myself dead.

Perhaps he accepts of this embassy on purpose that he may leave me and take another person with him: or perhaps, dearest mother (I hardly dare to hope it)—perhaps he wishes to break off that connexion, and goes to Russia to leave temptation behind him. I know that this embassy was offered to him some weeks ago, and he had then no thoughts of accepting it.—Oh that I could see into his heart—that heart which used to be always open to me! If I could discover what his wishes are, I should know what mine ought to be. I have thoughts of going to town immediately to see him; at least I may take leave of him. Do you approve of it? Write the moment you receive this; but I need not say that, for I am sure you will do so. Dearest mother, you have prophesied that his heart will return to me, and on this hope I live.

Your ever affectionate daughter,

LEONORA L—.

LETTER LXIV

THE DUCHESS OF — TO LEONORA.

Yes, my dear, I advise you by all means to go to town, and to see your husband. Your desire to accompany him to Russia he will know before you see him, for I have just written and despatched an express to him with your last letter, and with all those which I have received from you within these last six months. Leave Mr. L— time to read them before he sees you; and do not hurry or fatigue yourself unnecessarily. You know that an embassy cannot be arranged in two days; therefore travel by easy journeys: you cannot do otherwise without hazard. Your courage in offering to undertake this long voyage with your husband is worthy of you, my beloved daughter. God bless and preserve you! If you go to Petersburg, let me know in time, that I may see you before you leave England. I will be at any moment at any place you appoint.

Your affectionate mother,

—.

LETTER LXV

THE DUCHESS OF — TO MR. L—.

Perhaps this letter may find you at the feet of your mistress. Spare me, sir, a few moments from your pleasures. You may perhaps expect reproaches from the mother of your wife; but let me assure you, that you have none to apprehend. For my daughter's sake, if not for yours, I would forbear. Never was departing love recalled by the voice of reproach; you shall not hear it from me, you have not heard it from Leonora. But mistake not the cause of her forbearance; let it not be attributed to pusillanimity of temper, or insensibility of heart.

Enclosed I send you all the letters which my daughter has written to me from the first day of her acquaintance with Lady Olivia to this hour. From these you will be enabled to judge of what she has felt for some months past, and of the actual state of her heart; you will see all the tenderness and all the strength of her soul.

It has ever been my fixed opinion, that a wife who loves her husband, and who has possessed his affections, may reclaim them from the lure of the most artful of her sex, by persevering kindness, temper, and good sense, unless indeed her husband be a fool or a libertine. I have prophesied that my daughter will regain your heart; and upon this prophecy, to use her own expression, she lives. And even now, when its accomplishment is far removed, I am so steady in my opinion of her and of you; so convinced of the uniform result of certain conduct upon the human mind, that undismayed I repeat my prophecy.

Were you to remain in this kingdom, I should leave things to their natural course; I should not interfere so far even as to send you Leonora's letters: but as you may be separated for years, I think it necessary now to put into your hands incontrovertible proofs of what she is, and what she has been. Do not imagine that I am so weak as to expect that the perusal of these letters will work a sudden change: but it is fit that, before you leave England, you should know that Leonora is not a cold, sullen, or offended wife; but one who loves you most tenderly, most generously; who, concealing the agony of her heart, waits with resignation for the time when she will be your refuge, and the permanent blessing of your life.

—.

MADAME DE P— TO OLIVIA.

Paris.

And now, my charming Olivia, raise your fine eyes as high as ambition can look, and you will perhaps discover my grand object. You do not see it yet. Look again.—Do you not see the Emperor of Russia? What would you think of him for a lover? If it were only for novelty's sake, it would really be pleasant to have a Czar at one's feet. Reign in his heart, and you in fact seat yourself invisibly on the throne of all the Russias: thence what a commanding prospect you have of the affairs of Europe! and how we should govern the world at our ease! The project is bold, but not impracticable. The ancients represent Cupid riding the Numidian lion; and why should he not tame the Russian bear? It would make a pretty design for a vignette. I can engrave as well as La Pompadour could at least, and anticipating your victory, my charming Olivia, I will engrave Cupid leading the bear in a chain of flowers. This shall be my seal. Mon cachet de faveur.

Courage, my fair politician! You have a difficult task; but the glory is in proportion to the labour; and those who value power properly, are paid by its acquisition, for all possible fatigue and hardships. With your knowledge of our modes, you will be at Petersburg the arbitress of delights. You have a charming taste and invention for fetes and spectacles. Teach these people to vary their pleasures. Their monarch must adore you, if you banish from his presence that most dreadful enemy of kings, and most obstinate resident of courts, ennui. Trust, my Olivia, neither to your wit, nor your beauty, nor your accomplishments, but employ your "various arts of trifling prettily," and, take my word for it, you will succeed.

As I may not have an opportunity of sending you another private letter, and as lemon-juice, goulard, and all those sympathetic inks, are subject to unlucky accidents, I must send you all my secret instructions by the present safe conveyance.

You must absolutely sacrifice, my dear child, all your romantic notions, and all your taste for love, to the grand object. The Czar must not have the slightest cause for jealousy. These Czars make nothing, you know, of cutting off their mistresses' pretty heads upon the bare suspicion of an intrigue. But you must do what is still more difficult than to be constant, you must yield your will, and, what is more, you must never let this Czar guess that his will is not always your pleasure. Your humour, your tastes, your wishes, must be incessantly and with alacrity sacrificed to his. You must submit to the constraint of eternal court ceremony, and court dissimulation. You must bear to be surrounded with masks, instead of the human face divine; and instead of fellow-creatures, you must content yourself with puppets. You will have the amusement of pulling the wires: but remember that you must wear a mask perpetually as well as others, and never attempt to speak, and never expect to hear the language of truth or of the heart. You must not be the dupe of attachment in those who call themselves friends, or zealous and affectionate servants, &c. &c. You must have sufficient strength of character to bear continually in mind that all these professions are mere words, that all these people are alike false, and actuated but by one motive, self-interest. To secure yourself from secret and open enemies, you must farther have sufficient courage to live without a friend or a confidante, for such persons at court are only spies, traitors in the worst forms. All this is melancholy and provoking, to be sure; but all this you must see without feeling, or at least without showing a spark of indignation. A sentimental misanthropist, male or female, is quite out of place at court. You must see all that is odious and despicable in human nature in a comic point of view; and you must consider your fellow-creatures as objects to be laughed at, not to be hated. Laughter, besides being good for the health, and consequently for the complexion, always implies superiority. Without this gratification to our vanity, there would be no possibility of enduring that eternal penance of hypocrisy, and that solitary state of suspicion, to which the ambitious condemn themselves. I fear, my romantic Olivia, that you, who are a person used to yield to first impressions, and not quite accustomed to subdue your passions to your interest, will think that politics require too much from you, almost as much as constancy or religion. But consider the difference! for Heaven's sake, my dear, consider the greatness of our object! Would to God that I had the eloquence of Bossuet! and I would make you a convert from love and a proselyte to glory. Dare, my Olivia, to be a martyr to ambition!—See! already high in air she holds a crown over your head—it is almost within your grasp—stretch out your white arm and seize it—fear not the thorns!—every crown has thorns—but who upon that account ever yet refused one? My dear empress, I have the honour to kiss your powerful hands.

GABRIELLE DE P—.

MR. L— TO GENERAL B—.

MY DEAR FRIEND,

You need not hurry yourself to come to town on my account, for by this change of ministry my embassy will be delayed some weeks.

A few days ago this delay would have been a terrible disappointment to me; yet now I feel it a respite. A respite! you will exclaim. Yes, my dear friend—so it is. Such is the heart of man!—so changeable, so contradictory, so much at variance with itself from day to day, from hour to hour. I believe, from what I now feel, that every man under the dominion of passion is reduced to a most absurd and miserable condition.—I have just been reading some letters from Leonora, which have wrung my heart; letters addressed to her mother, laying open every feeling of her mind for some months. My dear friend, what injustice have I done to this admirable woman! With what tenderness, with what delicacy has she loved me! while I, mistaking modesty for coldness, fortitude for indifference, have neglected, injured, and abandoned her! With what sweetness of temper, with what persevering goodness has she borne with me, while, intoxicated with passion, I saw every thing in a false point of view! How often have I satisfied myself with the persuasion, that she scarcely observed my attachment to Olivia, or beheld it unconcerned, secure by the absence of love from the pangs of jealousy! How often have I accused her of insensibility, whilst her heart was in tortures! Olivia was deceived also, and confirmed me in this cruel error. And all that time Leonora was defending her rival, and pleading her cause! With what generosity, with what magnanimity she speaks of Olivia in those letters! Her confidence was unbounded, her soul above suspicion; to the very last she doubted and blamed herself—dear, amiable woman! blamed herself for our faults, for feeling that jealousy, which no wife who loved as she did could possibly subdue. She never betrayed it by a single word or look of reproach. Even though she fainted at that cursed fête champêtre, yet the moment she came to her senses, she managed so, that none of the spectators could suspect she thought Olivia was her rival. My dear general, you will forgive me—as long as I praise Leonora you will understand me. At last you will acknowledge that I do justice to the merits of my wife. Justice! no—I am unworthy of her. I have no heart like hers to offer in return for such love. She wishes to go with me to Petersburg; she has forborne to make this offer directly to me; but I know it from her last letter to her mother, which now lies before me. How can I refuse?—and how can I accept? My soul is torn with violence different ways. How can I leave Leonora! and how can I tear myself from Olivia!—even if her charms had no power over my heart, how could I with honour desert the woman who has sacrificed every thing for me! I will not shield myself from you, my friend, behind the word honour. See me as you have always seen me, without disguise, and now without defence. I respect, I love Leonora—but, alas! I am in love with Olivia!

Yours ever,

F. L—.

LETTER LXVIII

MR. L— TO OLIVIA.

Triumphant as you are over my heart, dear enchanting Olivia! you cannot make me false. I cannot, even to appease your anger, deny this morning what I said last night. It is inconsistent with all your professions, with your character, with your generous disposition, to desire me to "abjure Leonora for ever!" it would be to render myself for ever unworthy of Olivia. I am convinced that had you read the letters of which I spoke, you would have been touched, you would have been struck by them as I was: instead of being hurt and displeased by the impression that they made upon me, you would have sympathized in my feelings, you would have been indignant if I had not admired, you would have detested and despised me if I could have been insensible to "so much goodness and generosity." I repeat my words: I will not "retract," I cannot "repent of them." My dear Olivia! when you reflect upon what is past, I am persuaded you will acknowledge that your sensibility made you unjust. Indeed, my love, you did not show your usual candour; I had just read all that Leonora had written of you, all that she had urged against her mother in your defence; even when she had most cause to be irritated against us, I could not avoid being shocked by the different manner in which you spoke of her. Perhaps I told you so too abruptly: if I had loved you less, I should have been more cautious and more calm—if I had esteemed you less, calmer still. I could then, possibly, have borne to hear you speak in a manner unbecoming yourself. Forgive me the pain I gave you—the pain I now give you, my dearest Olivia! My sincerity is the best security you can have for my future love. Banish therefore this unjust, this causeless jealousy: moderate this excessive sensibility for both our sakes, and depend upon the power you have over my heart. You cannot conceive how much I have felt from this misunderstanding—the first we have ever had. Let it be the last. I have spent a sleepless night. I am detained in town by provoking, tiresome, but necessary business. Meet me in the evening with smiles, my Olivia: let me behold in those fascinating eyes their wonted expression, and hear from your voice its usual, its natural tone of tenderness and love.

Ever devotedly yours,

F. L—.

OLIVIA TO MR. L—.

You have spoken daggers to me! Come not to Richmond this evening! I cannot—will not see you! Not for the universe would I see you with my present feelings!

Write to me more letters like that which I have just received. Dip your pen in gall; find words more bitter than those which you have already used. Accuse me of want of candour, want of generosity, want of every amiable, every estimable quality. Upbraid me with the loss of all of which you have bereft me. Recollect every sacrifice that I have made, and, if you can, imagine every sacrifice that I would still make for you—peace of mind, friends, country, fortune, fame, virtue; name them all, and triumph—and disdain your triumph! Remind me how low I am fallen—sink me lower still—insult, debase, humble me to the dust. Exalt my rival, unroll to my aching eyes the emblazoned catalogue of her merits, her claims to your esteem, your affection; number them over, dwell upon those that I have forfeited, those which can never be regained; tell me that such merits are above all price; assure me that beyond all her sex you respect, you admire, you love your wife; say it with enthusiasm, with fire in your eyes, with all the energy of passion in your voice; then bid me sympathize in your feelings—bid me banish jealousy—wonder at my alarm—call my sorrow anger—conjure me to restrain my sensibility! Restrain my sensibility! Unhappy Olivia! he is tired of your love. Let him then at once tell me the dreadful truth, and I will bear it. Any evil is better than uncertainty, than lingering hope. Drive all hope from my mind. Bid me despair and die—but do not stretch me on the rack of jealousy!—Yet if such be your cruel pleasure, enjoy it.—Determine how much I can endure and live. Stop just at the point where human nature sinks, that you may not lose your victim, that she may linger on from day to day, your sport and your derision.

OLIVIA.

MR. L— TO GENERAL B—.

My Dear General,

You will rejoice to hear that Olivia and I have been in a state of warfare for some days past, and you will be still more pleased when you learn the cause of our quarrel. On the day that I had been reading Leonora's letters I was rather later at Richmond than usual. Olivia, offended, insisted upon knowing by what I could possibly have been detained. Her anger knew no bounds when she heard the truth. She made use of some expressions, in speaking of my wife, which I could not, I hope, have borne at any time, but which shocked me beyond measure at that moment. I defended Leonora with warmth. Olivia, in a scornful tone, talked of my wife's coldness of disposition, and bid me compare Lady Leonora's love with hers. It was a comparison I had it more in my power to make than Olivia was aware of; it was the most disadvantageous moment for her in which that comparison could be made. She saw or suspected my feelings, and perceived that all she had said of my Leonora's incapability of loving produced an effect directly contrary to her expectations. Transported by jealousy, she then threw out hints respecting the Prince. I spoke as I felt, indignantly. I know not precisely what I said, but Olivia and I parted in anger. I have since received a passionately fond note from her. But I feel unhappy. Dear general, when will you come to town?

Yours truly,

F. L—

LETTER LXXI

MRS. C— TO THE DUCHESS OF —.

MY DEAR MADAM,

Your grace's cautions and entreaties to Lady Leonora not to over-exert and fatigue herself were, alas! as ineffectual as mine. From the time she heard that Mr. L— had accepted this embassy to Petersburg, she was so eager to set out on her journey to town, and so impatient to see him, that neither her mind nor her body had one moment's tranquillity. She waited with indescribable anxiety for your grace's answer to her letter; and the instant she was secure of your approbation, her carriage was ordered to the door. I saw that she was ill; but she would not listen to my fears; she repeated with triumph, that her mother made no objection to her journey, and that she had no apprehensions for herself. However, she was obliged at last to yield. The carriage was actually at the door, when she was forced to submit to be carried to her bed. For several hours she was in such danger, that I never expected she could live till this day. Thank God! she is now safe. Her infant, to her great delight, is a boy: she was extremely anxious to have a son, because Mr. L— formerly wished for one so much. She forbids me to write to Mr. L—, lest I should communicate the account of her sudden illness too abruptly.

She particularly requests that your grace will mention to him this accident in the least alarming manner possible. I shall write again next post. Lady Leonora has now fallen asleep, and seems to sleep quietly. Who should sleep in peace if she cannot? I never saw her equal,

My dear madam,

I am,

With respect and attachment,

Your grace's

Sincerely affectionate,

HELEN C—.

It is with extreme concern I am forced to add, that since I wrote this letter the child has been so ill that I have fears for his life.—His poor mother!

LETTER LXXII

MR. L— TO GENERAL B—.

MY DEAR GENERAL,

All is upon velvet again. Poor Olivia was excessively hurt by my letter: she was ill for two days—seriously ill. Yesterday I at length obtained admittance. Olivia was all softness, all candour: she acknowledged that she had been wrong, and in so sweet a voice! She blamed herself till I could no longer think her blamable. She seemed so much humbled and depressed, such a tender melancholy appeared in her bewitching eyes, that I could not resist the fascination. I certainly gave her some cause for displeasure that unfortunate evening; for as Olivia has strong passions and exquisite sensibility, I should not have been so abrupt. A fit of jealousy may seize the best and most generous mind, and may prompt to what it would be incapable of saying or thinking in dispassionate moments. I am sure that Olivia has, upon reflection, felt more pain from this affair than I have. My Russian embassy is still in abeyance. Ministers seem to know their own minds as little as I know mine. Ambition has its quarrels and follies as well as love. At all events, I shall not leave England till next month; and I shall not go down to L— Castle till I have received my last instructions from our court, and till the day for my sailing is fixed. The parting with Leonora will be a dreadful difficulty. I cannot think of it steadily. But as she herself says, "is it not better that she should lose a year of my affections than a life?" The Duchess is mistaken in imagining it possible that any woman, let her influence be ever so great over my heart, could prejudice me against my amiable, my admirable wife. What has just passed between Olivia and me, convinces me that it is impossible. She has too much knowledge of my character to hazard in future a similar attempt. No, my dear friend, be assured I would not suffer it. I have not yet lost all title to your esteem or to my own. This enchantress may intoxicate me with her cup, but shall never degrade me; and I should feel myself less degraded even by losing the human form than by forfeiting that principle of honour and virtue, which more nobly distinguishes man from brute.

Yours most sincerely,

F. L—.

LETTER LXXIII

GENERAL B— TO MR. L—.

MY DEAR FRIEND,

It is well that I did not answer your letter of Saturday before I received that of Monday. My congratulations upon your quarrel with your fair one might have come just as you were kissing hands upon a reconciliation.

I have often found a great convenience in writing a bad hand; my letters are so little like what they are intended for, and have among them such equality of unintelligibility, that each seems either; and with the slightest alteration, each will stand and serve for the other. My m, n, and u, are convertible letters; so are the terms and propositions of your present mode of reasoning, my dear L—, and I perceive that you find your account in it. Upon this I congratulate you; and I congratulate Lady Leonora upon your being detained some weeks longer in England. Those who have a just cause need never pray for victory; they need only ask the gods for time. Time always brings victory to truth, and shame to falsehood. But you are not worthy of such fine apophthegms. At present "you are not fit to hear yourself convinced." I will wait for a better opportunity, and have patience with you, if I can.

You seem to plume yourself mightily upon your resolve to do justice to the merits of your wife, and upon the courage you have shown in stuffing cotton into your ears to prevent your listening to the voice of the siren: but pray take the cotton out, and hear all she can say or sing. Lady Leonora cannot be hurt by any thing Olivia can say, but her own malice may destroy herself.

In the mean time, as you tell me that you are upon velvet again, I am to presume that you are perfectly at ease; and I should be obliged to you, if, as often as you can find leisure, you would send me bulletins of your happiness. I have never yet been in love with one of these high-flown heroines, and I am really curious to know what degree of felicity they can bestow upon a man of common sense. I should be glad to benefit by the experience of a friend.

Yours truly,

J.B.

LETTER LXXIV

OLIVIA TO MADAME DE P—.

Richmond.

Accept my sincere thanks, inimitable Gabrielle! for having taken off my hands a lover, who really has half-wearied me to death. If you had dealt more frankly with me, I could, however, have saved you much superfluous trouble and artifice. I now perfectly comprehend the cause of poor R—'s strange silence some months ago; he was then under the influence of your charms, and it was your pleasure to deceive me even when there was no necessity for dissimulation. You knew the secret of my growing attachment to L—, and must have foreseen that R— would be burthensome to me. You needed therefore only to have treated me with candour, and you would have gained a lover without losing a friend: but Madame de P— is too accomplished a politician to go the simple straight road to her object. I now perfectly comprehend why she took such pains to persuade me that an imperial lover was alone worthy of my charms. She was alarmed by an imaginary danger. Believe me, I am incapable of disputing with any one les restes d'un coeur.

Permit me to assure you, madam, that your incomparable talents for explanation will be utterly thrown away on me in future. I am in possession of the whole truth, from a person whose information I cannot doubt: I know the precise date of the commencement of your connexion with R—, so that you must perceive it will be impracticable to make me believe that you have not betrayed my easy confidence.

I cannot, however, without those pangs of sentiment which your heart will never experience, reflect upon the treachery, the perfidy of one who has been my bosom friend.—Return my letters, Gabrielle.— With this you will receive certain souvenirs, at which I could never henceforward look without sighing. I return you that ring I have so long worn with delight, the picture of that treacherous eye,[*] which you know so well how to use.—Adieu, Gabrielle.—The illusion is over.—How many of the illusions of my fond heart have been dispelled by time and treachery!

OLIVIA.

[*Certain ladies at this time carried pictures of the eyes of their favourites.]

LETTER LXXV

MADAME DE P— TO MONSIEUR R—.

Paris, — 18, —.

I have just received the most extravagant letter imaginable from your Olivia. Really you may congratulate yourself, my dear friend, upon having recovered your liberty. 'Twere better to be a galley slave at once than to be bound to please a woman for life, who knows not what she would have either in love or friendship. Can you conceive anything so absurd as her upbraiding me with treachery, because I know the value of a heart, of which she tells me she was more than half tired? as if I were to blame for her falling in love with Mr. L—, and as if I did not know the whole progress of her inconstancy. Her letters to me give a new history of the birth and education of Love. Here we see Love born of Envy, nursed by Ennui, and dandled in turn by all the Vices.

And this Lady Olivia fancies that she is a perfect French woman! There is nothing we Parisians abhor and ridicule so much as these foreign, and always awkward, caricatures of our manners. With us there are many who, according to a delicate distinction, lose their virtue without losing their taste for virtue; but I flatter myself there are few who resemble Olivia entirely—who have neither the virtues of a man nor of a woman. One cannot even say that "her head is the dupe of her heart," since she has no heart. But enough of such a tiresome and incomprehensible subject.

How I overvalued that head, when I thought it could ever be fit for politics! 'Tis well we did not commit ourselves. You see how prudent I am, my dear R—, and how much those are mistaken who think that we women are not fit to be trusted with secrets of state. Love and politics make the best mixture in the world. Adieu. Victoire summons me to my toilette.

GABRIELLE DE P—.

MADAME DE P— TO LADY OLIVIA.

Paris,— 18, —.

Really, my dear Olivia, this is too childish. What! make a complaint in form against me for taking a lover off your hands when you did not know what to do with him! Do you quarrel in England every time you change partners in a country dance? But I must be serious; for the high-sounding words treachery and perfidy are surely sufficient to make any body grave. Seriously, then, if you are resolved to be tragical, et de me faire une scene, I must submit—console myself, and, above all things, take care not to be ridiculous.

Your letters, as you desire it so earnestly, and with so much reason, shall be returned by the first safe conveyance; but excuse me if I forbear to restore your souvenirs. With us Parisians, this returning of keepsakes has been out of fashion, since the days of Moliere and Le dépit amoureux.

Adieu, my charming Olivia! I embrace you tenderly, I was going to say; but I believe, according to your English etiquette, I must now conclude with

I have the honour to be,

Madam,

Your most obedient,

Humble servant,

GABRIELLE DE P—.

FROM OLIVIA TO MR. L—.

Tuesday morning.

Come not to Richmond to-day; I am not in spirits to see you, my dearest L—. Allow me to indulge my melancholy retired from every human eye.

OLIVIA.

FROM LADY OLIVIA TO MR. L—.

Tuesday evening.

"Explain to you the cause of my melancholy "—Vain request!—cruel as vain! Your ignorance of the cause too well justifies my sad presentiments. Were our feelings in unison, as once they were, would not every chord of your heart vibrate responsively to mine?

With me, love is an absorbing vortex of the soul, into which all other thoughts, feelings, and ideas are irresistibly impelled; with you, it is but as the stranger stream that crosses the peaceful lake, and, as it flows, wakens only the surface of the slumbering waters, communicating to them but a temporary agitation. With you, my dear, but too tranquil-minded friend, love is but one amid the vulgar crowd of pleasures; it concentrates not your ideas, it entrances not your faculties; it is not, as in my heart, the supreme delight, which renders all others tasteless, the only blessing which can make life supportable; the sole, sufficient object of existence. Alas! how cruelly different is the feeble attachment that I have inspired from that all-powerful sentiment to which I live a victim! Countless symptoms, by you unheeded, mark to my love-watchful eye the decline of passion. How often am I secretly shocked by the cold carelessness of your words and manner! How often does the sigh burst from my bosom, the tear fall from my eye, when you have left me at leisure to recall, by memory's torturing power, instances of your increasing indifference! Seek not to calm my too well-founded fears. Professions, with all their unmeaning, inanimate formality, but irritate my anguish. Permit me to indulge, to feed upon my grief in silence. Ask me no more to explain to you the cause of my melancholy. Too plainly, alas! I feel it is beyond my utmost power to endure it. Amiable Werter—divine St. Preux—you would sympathize in my feelings! Sublime Goethe—all-eloquent Rousseau—you alone could feel as I do, and you alone could paint my anguish.

The miserable

OLIVIA.

MR. L— TO GENERAL B—.

Expect no bulletin of happiness from me, my friend. I find it impossible to make Olivia happy. She has superior talents, accomplishments, beauty, grace, all that can attract and fascinate the human heart— that could triumph over every feeling, every principle that opposed her power: she lives with the man she loves, and yet she is miserable.

Rousseau, it has been said, never really loved any woman but his own Julie; I have lately been tempted to think that Olivia never really loved any man but St. Preux. Werter, perhaps, and some other German heroes, might dispute her heart even with St. Preux; but as for me, I begin to be aware that I am loved only as a feeble resemblance of those divine originals (to whom, however, my character bears not the slightest similarity), and I am often indirectly, and sometimes directly, reproached with my inferiority to imaginary models. But how can a plain Englishman hope to reach

"The high sublime of deep absurd?"

I am continually reviled for not using a romantic language, which I have never learned; and which, as far as I can judge, is foreign to all natural feeling. I wish to make Olivia happy. There is nothing I would not do to satisfy her of my sincerity; but nothing I can do will suffice. She has a sort of morbid sensibility, which is more alive to pain than pleasure, more susceptible of jealousy than of love. No terms are sufficiently strong to convince her of my affection, but an unguarded word makes her miserable for hours. She requires to be agitated by violent emotions, though they exhaust her mind, and leave her spiritless and discontented. In this alternation of rapture and despair all her time passes. As she says of herself, she has no soul but for love: she seems to think it a crime against sentiment, to admit of relief from common occupations or indifferent subjects; with a sort of superstitious zeal, she excludes all thoughts but those which relate to one object, and in this spirit of amorous mysticism she actually makes a penance even of love. I am astonished that her heart can endure this variety of self-inflicted torments. What will become of Olivia when she ceases to love and be loved? And what passion can be durable which is so violent as hers, and to which no respite is allowed? No affection can sustain these hourly trials of suspicion and reproach.

Jealousy of Leonora has taken such possession of Olivia's imagination, that she misinterprets all my words and actions. By restraining my thoughts, by throwing obstacles in the way of my affection for my wife, she stimulates and increases it: she forces upon me continually those comparisons which she dreads. Till I knew Olivia more intimately than the common forms of a first acquaintance, or the illusions of a treacherous passion permitted, her defects did not appear; but now that I suffer, and that I see her suffer daily, I deplore them bitterly. Her happiness rests and weighs heavily on my honour. I feel myself bound to consider and to provide for the happiness of the woman who has sacrificed to me all independent means of felicity. A man without honour or humanity may perhaps finish an intrigue as easily as he can begin it, but this is not exactly the case of your imprudent friend,

F. L—.

LETTER LXXX

GENERAL B— TO MR. L—.

Wednesday.

AY, ay! just as I thought it would be. This is all the comfort, my dear friend, that I can give you; all the comfort that wise people usually afford their friends in distress. Provided things happen just as they predicted, they care but little what is suffered in the accomplishment of their prophecies. But seriously, my dear L—, I am not sorry that you are in a course of vexation. The more you see of your charmer the better. She will allay your intoxication by gentle degrees, and send you sober home. Pray keep in the course you have begun, and preserve your patience as long as possible. I should be sorry that you and Olivia quarrelled violently, and parted in a passion: such quarrels of lovers are proverbially the renewal of love.

"Il faut délier l'amitie, il faut couper l'amour."

In some cases this maxim may be just, but not in the present instance. I would rather wait till the knot is untied than cut it; for when once you see the art with which it was woven, a similar knot can never again perplex you.

Yours truly,

J. B.

FROM OLIVIA TO MR. L—.

Richmond, Saturday.

You presume too much upon your power over my heart, and upon the softness of my nature. Know that I have spirit as well as tenderness—a spirit that will neither be injured nor insulted with impunity. You were amazed, you say, by the violence which I showed yesterday. Why did you provoke that violence by opposing the warmest wish of my heart, and with a calmness that excited my tenfold indignation? Imagine not that I am a tame, subjugated female, to be treated with neglect if I remonstrate, and caressed as the price of obedience. Fancy not that I am one of your chimney-corner, household goddesses, doomed to the dull uniformity of domestic worship, destined to to be adored, to be hung with garlands, or undeified or degraded with indignity! I have been accustomed to a different species of worship; and the fondness of my weak heart has not yet sunk me so low, and rendered me so abject, that I cannot assert my rights. You tell me that you are unconscious of giving me any just cause of offence. Just cause!—How I hate the cold accuracy of your words! This single expression is sufficient offence to a heart like mine. You entreat me to be reasonable. Reasonable!—did ever man talk of reason to a woman he loved? When once a man has recourse to reason and precision, there is an end of love. No just cause of offence!—What, have I no cause to be indignant, when I find you thus trifle with my feelings, postpone from week to week, and month to month, our departure from this hateful country—

"Bid me hope on from day to day, And wish and wish my soul away!"

Yes, you know it to be the most ardent wish of my soul to leave England; you know that I cannot enjoy a moment's peace of mind whilst I am here; yet in this racking suspense it is your pleasure to detain me. No, it shall not be—this shall not go on! It is in vain you tell me that the delay originates not with you, that you must wait for instructions, and I know not what—paltry diplomatic excuses!

OLIVIA.

MR. L— TO GENERAL B—.

Richmond.

Amuse yourself, my good general, at my expense; I know that you are seriously interested for my happiness; but the way is not quite so clear before me as you imagine. It is extremely easy to be philosophic for our friends; but difficult to be so for ourselves when our passions are concerned. Indeed, this would be a contradiction in terms; you might as well talk of a cold sun, or of hot ice, as of a philosopher falling in love, or of a man in love being a philosopher. You say that Olivia will wear out my passion, and that her defects will undo the work of her charms. I acknowledge that she sometimes ravels the web she has woven; but she is miraculously expeditious and skilful in repairing the mischief: the magical tissue again appears firm as ever, glowing with brighter colours, and exhibiting finer forms.

In plain prose, my dear friend—for as you ate not in love, you will find it difficult to follow my poetic nights—in plain prose, I must confess that Olivia has the power to charm and touch my heart, even after she has provoked me to the utmost verge of human patience. She knows her power, and I am afraid this tempts her to abuse it. Her temper, which formerly appeared to me all feminine gentleness, is now irritable and violent; but I am persuaded that this is not her natural disposition; it is the effect of her present unhappy state of mind. Tortured by remorse and jealousy, if in the height of their paroxysms, Olivia make me suffer from their fury, is it for me to complain? I, who caused, should at least endure the evil.

Every thing is arranged for my embassy, and the day is fixed for our leaving England. I go down to L— Castle next week.

Your faithful

F. L—.

JOSEPHINE TO VICTOIRE, MAD. DE P—'s WOMAN.

Richmond.

I am in despair, dear Victoire; and unless your genius can assist me, absolutely undone! Here is this romantic lady of mine determined upon a journey to Russia with her new English lover. What whims ladies take into their heads, and how impossible it is to make them understand reason! I have been labouring in vain to convince my Lady Olivia that this is the most absurd scheme imaginable: and I have repeated to her all I learnt from Lady F—'s women, who are just returned from Petersburg, and whom I met at a party last night, all declaring they would rather die a thousand deaths, than go through again what they have endured. Such seas of ice! such going in sledges! such barbarians! such beds! and scarcely a looking-glass! And nothing fit to wear but what one carries with one, and God knows how long we may stay. At Petersburg the coachmen's ears are frozen off every night on their boxes waiting for their ladies. And there are bears and wild beasts, I am told, howling with their mouths wide open night and day in the forests which we are to pass through; and even in the towns, the men, I hear, are little better; for it is the law of the country for the men to beat their wives, and many wear long beards. How horrid!—My Lady F—'s woman, who is a Parisian born, and very pretty, if her eyes were not so small, and better dressed than her lady always, except diamonds, assures me, upon her honour, she never had a civil thing said to her whilst she was in Russia, except by one or two Frenchmen in the suite of the ambassadors.

These Russians think of nothing but drinking brandy, and they put pepper into it! Mon Dieu, what savages! Put pepper into brandy! But that is inconceivable! Positively, I will never go to Petersburg. And yet if my lady goes, what will become of me? for you know my sentiments for Brunel, and he is decided to accompany my lady, so I cannot stay behind.

But absolutely I am shocked at this intrigue with Mr. L—, and my conscience reproaches me terribly with being a party concerned in it; for in this country an affair of gallantry between married people is not so light a thing as with us. Here wives sometimes love their husbands seriously, as if they were their lovers; and my Lady Leonora L— is one of this sort of wives. She is very unhappy, I am told. One day at L— Castle, I assure you my heart quite bled for her, when she gave me a beautiful gown of English muslin, little suspecting me then to be her enemy. She is certainly very unsuspicious, and very amiable, and I wish to Heaven her husband would think as I do, and take her with him to Petersburg, instead of carrying off my Lady Olivia and me! Adieu, mon chou! Embrace every body I know, tenderly, for me.

Josephine.

LETTER LXXXIV

MRS. C— TO THE DUCHESS OF —.

MY DEAR MADAM,

I believe, when I wrote last to your grace, I said that I had no hopes of the child's life. From the moment of his birth there was but little probability of his being any thing but a source of misery to his mother. I cannot, on her account, regret that the struggle is over. He expired this morning. My poor friend had hopes to the last, though I had none; and it was most painful and alarming to see the feverish anxiety with which she watched over her little boy, frequently repeating, "Mr. L— used to wish so much for a son.—I hope the boy will live to see his father."

Last night, partly by persuasion, partly by compulsion, I prevailed with her to let the child be taken out of her room. This morning, as soon as it was light, I heard her bell ring; the poor little thing was at that moment in convulsions; and knowing that Lady Leonora rang to inquire for it, I went to prepare her mind for what I knew must be the event. The moment I came into the room she looked eagerly in my face, but did not ask me any questions about the child. I sat down by the side of her bed; but without listening to what I said about her own health, she rang her bell again more violently than before. Susan came in. "Susan!—without my child!"—said she, starting up. Susan hesitated, but I saw by her countenance that it was all over—so did Lady Leonora. She said not a word, but drawing her curtain suddenly, she lay down, and never spoke or stirred for three hours. The first words she said afterwards were to me:

"You need not move so softly, my dear Helen; I am not asleep. Have you my mother's last letter? I think my mother says that she will be here to-morrow? She is very kind to come to me. Will you be so good as to write to her immediately, and send a servant with your letter as soon as you can to meet her on the road, that she may not be surprised when she arrives?"

Lady Leonora is now more composed and more like herself than she has been for some time past. I rejoice that your Grace will so soon be here, because you will be her best possible consolation; and I do not know any other person in the world who could have sufficient influence to prevent her from attempting to set out upon a journey before she can travel with safety. To do her justice, she has not hinted that such were her intentions; but still I know her mind so well, that I am certain what her thoughts are, and what her actions would be. Most ladies talk more than they act, but Leonora acts more decidedly than she talks.

Believe, me, dear madam,

With much respect,

Your Grace's

Sincerely affectionate

HELEN C—.

LETTER LXXXV

MR. L— TO GENERAL B—.

I thank you, my excellent friend, for the kindness of your last letter [*], which came to me at the time I wanted it most. In the whole course of my life, I never felt so much self-reproach, as I have done since I heard of the illness of Leonora and the loss of my son. From this blow my mind will not easily recover. Of all torments self-reproach is the worst. And even now I cannot follow the dictates of my own heart, and of my better judgment.

In Olivia's company I am compelled to repress my feelings; she cannot sympathize in them; they offend her: she is dissatisfied even with my silence, and complains of my being out of spirits. Out of spirits!— How can I be otherwise at present? Has Olivia no touch of pity for a woman who was once her friend, who always treated her with generous kindness? But perhaps I am a little unreasonable, and expect too much from female nature.

At all events, I wish that Olivia would spare me at this moment her sentimental metaphysics. She is for ever attempting to prove to me that I cannot love so well as she can. I admit that I cannot talk of love so finely. I hope all this will not go on when we arrive at Petersburg.

The ministry at last know their own minds. I saw — to-day, and every thing will be quickly arranged; therefore, my dear friend, do not delay coming to town, to

Your obliged

F. L—.

*[*This letter does not appear.]*

GENERAL B— TO MR. L—.

Perhaps you are a little unreasonable! Indeed, my dear friend, I do not think you a little unreasonable, but very nearly stark mad. What! quarrel with your mistress because she is not sorry that your wife is ill, and because she cannot sympathize in your grief for the loss of your son! Where, except perhaps in absurd novels, did you ever meet with these paragons of mistresses, who were so magnanimous and so generous as to sacrifice their own reputations, and then be satisfied to share the only possible good remaining to them in life, the heart of their lover, with a rival more estimable, more amiable than themselves, and who has the advantage of being a wife? This sharing of hearts, this union of souls, with this opposition of interests—this metaphysical gallantry is absolute nonsense, and all who try it in real life will find it so to their cost. Why should you, my dear L—, expect such superlative excellence from your Olivia? Do you think that a woman by losing one virtue increases the strength of those that remain, as it is said that the loss of one of our senses renders all the others more acute? Do you think that a lady, by yielding to love, and by proving that she has not sufficient resolution or forbearance to preserve the honour of her sex, gives the best possible demonstration of her having sufficient strength of character to rise superior to all the other weaknesses incident to human, and more especially to female nature— envy and jealousy for instance?

No, no, my good friend, you have common sense, though you lately have been sparing of it in action. You had a wife, and a good wife, and you had some chance of being happy; but with a wife and a mistress, granting them to be both the best of their kind, the probabilities are rather against you. I speak only as a man of the world: morality, you know, is now merely an affair of calculation. According to the most approved tables of happiness, you have made a bad bargain. But be just, at any rate, and do not blame your Olivia for the inconveniences and evils inseparable from the species of connexion that you have been pleased to form. Do you expect the whole course of society and the nature of the human heart to change for your special accommodation? Do you believe in truth by wholesale, and yet in detail expect a happy exception in your own favour?—Seriously, my dear friend, you must either break off this connexion, or bear it. I shall see you in a few days.

Yours truly,

J. B.

MRS C— TO MISS B—

L— Castle.

Leonora has recovered her strength surprisingly. She was so determined to be well, that her body dared not contradict her mind. Her excellent mother has been of the greatest possible service to us, for she has had sufficient influence to prevent her daughter from exerting herself too much. Her Grace had a letter from Mr. L— to-day—very short, but very kind—at least all that I heard read of it. He has set my heart somewhat more at ease by the comfortable assurance, that he will not leave England without seeing Lady Leonora. I have the greatest hopes from this interview! I have not felt so happy for many months—but I will not be too sanguine. Mr. L— talks of being here the latter end of this month. The duchess, with her usual prudence, intends to leave her daughter before that time, lest Mr. L— should be constrained by her presence, or should imagine that Leonora acts from any impulse but that of her own heart. I also, though much against my inclination, shall decamp; for he might perhaps consider me as an adviser, caballer, confidante, or at least a troublesome spectator. All reconciliation scenes should be without spectators. Men do not like to be seen on their knees: they are at a loss, like Sir Walter Raleigh in "The Critic;" they cannot get off gracefully. I am, dear Margaret,

Yours affectionately,

HELEN C—.

GENERAL B— TO MR. L—.

MY DEAR L—, Friday.

Ask yourself, in the name of common sense, why you should go to Petersburg with this sentimental coquette, this romantic termagant, of whom I see you are already more than half tired. As to your being bound to her in honour, I cannot see how. Why should you make honour, justice, humanity, and gratitude, plead so finely all on one side, and that the wrong side of the question? Have none of these one word to whisper in favour of any body in this world but of a worthless mistress, who makes you miserable? I think you have learned from your heroine to be so expert in sentimental logic, that you can change virtues into vices, and vices into virtues, till at last you do not know them asunder. Else why should you make it a point of conscience to abandon your wife—just at the moment, too, when you are thoroughly convinced of her love for you, when you are touched to the soul by her generous conduct, and when your heart longs to return to her?

Please to remember that this Lady Olivia's reputation was not unimpeached before her acquaintance with you, and do not take more glory or more blame to yourself than properly falls to your share. Do not forget that poor R— was your predecessor, and do not let this delicate lady rest all the weight of her shame upon you, as certain Chinese culprits rest their portable pillories on the shoulders of their friends.

In two days I shall follow this letter, and repeat in person all the interrogatories I have just put to you, my dear friend. Prepare yourself to answer me sincerely such questions as I shall ask.

Yours truly,

J.B.

LETTER LXXXIX

FROM OLIVIA TO MR. L—.

Monday, 12 o'clock.

For a few days did you say? To bid adieu? Oh! if once more you return to that fatal castle, that enchanted home, Olivia for ever loses all power over your heart. Bid her die, stab her to the heart, and she will call it mercy, and she will bless you with her dying lips; but talk not of leaving your Olivia! On her knees she writes this, her face all bathed in tears. And must she in her turn implore and supplicate? Must she abase herself even to the dust? Yes—love like hers vanquishes even the stubborn potency of female pride.

Your too fond

OLIVIA.

LETTER XC

FROM OLIVIA TO MR. L—.

[Dated a few hours after the preceding.]

Monday, half-past three.

Oh! this equivocating answer to my fond heart! Passion makes and admits of no compromise. Be mine, and wholly mine—or never, never will I survive your desertion! I can be happy only whilst I love; I can love only whilst I am beloved with fervency equal to my own; and when I cease to love, I cease to exist! No coward fears restrain my soul. The word suicide shocks not my ear, appals not my understanding. Death I consider but as the eternal rest of the wretched—the sweet, the sole refuge of despair.

Your resolute

OLIVIA.

LETTER XCI

FROM OLIVIA TO MR. L—.

Tuesday.

Return! return! on the wings of love return to the calm, the prudent, the happy, the transcendently happy Leonora! Return—but not to bid her adieu—return to be hers for ever, and only hers. I give you back your faith—I give you back your promises—you have taken back your heart.

But if you should desire once more to see Olivia, if you should have any lingering wish to bid her a last adieu, it must be this evening. To-morrow's sun rises not for Olivia. For her but a few short hours remain. Love, let them be all thy own! Intoxicate thy victim, mingle pleasure in the cup of death, and bid her fearless quaff it to the dregs!—

LETTER XCII

MR. L— TO GENERAL B—.

Thursday.

My Dear Friend,

You have by argument and raillery, and by every means that kindness and goodness could devise, endeavoured to expel from my mind a passion which you justly foresaw would be destructive of my happiness, and of the peace of a most estimable and amiable woman. With all the skill that a thorough knowledge of human nature in general, and of my peculiar character and foibles, could bestow, you have employed those

—"Words and spells which can control,

Between the fits, the fever of the soul."

Circumstances have operated in conjunction with your skill to "medicine me to repose." The fits have gradually become weaker and weaker, the fever is now gone, but I am still to suffer for the extravagances committed during its delirium. I have entered into engagements which must be fulfilled; I have involved myself in difficulties from which I see no method of extricating myself honourably. Notwithstanding all the latitude which the system of modern gallantry allows to the conscience of our sex, and in spite of the convenient maxim, which maintains that all arts are allowable in love and war, I think that a man cannot break a promise, whether made in words or by tacit implication, on the faith of which a woman sacrifices her reputation and happiness. Lady Olivia has thrown herself upon my protection. I am as sensible as you can be, my dear general, that scandal had attacked her reputation before our acquaintance commenced; but though the world had suspicions, they had no proofs: now there can be no longer any defence made for her character, there is no possibility of her returning to that rank in society to which she was entitled by her birth, and which she adorned with all the brilliant charms of wit and beauty; no happiness, no chance of happiness remains for her but from my constancy. Of naturally violent passions, unused to the control of authority, habit, reason, or religion, and at this time impelled by love and jealousy, Olivia is on the brink of despair. I am not apt to believe that women die in modern times for love, nor am I easily disposed to think that I could inspire a dangerous degree of enthusiasm; yet I am persuaded that Olivia's passion, compounded as it is of various sentiments besides love, has taken such possession of her imagination, and is, as she fancies, so necessary to her existence, that if I were to abandon her, she would destroy that life, which she has already attempted, I thank God! ineffectually. What a spectacle is a woman in a paroxysm of rage!—a woman we love, or whom we have loved!

Excuse me, my dear friend, if I wrote incoherently, for I have been interrupted many times since I began this letter. I am this day overwhelmed by a multiplicity of affairs, which, in consequence of Olivia's urgency to leave England immediately, must be settled with an expedition for which my head is not at present well qualified. I do not feel well: I can command my attention but on one subject, and on that all my thoughts are to no purpose. Whichever way I now act, I must endure and inflict misery. I must either part from a wife who has given me the most tender, the most touching proofs of affection—a wife who is all that a man can esteem, admire, and love; or I must abandon a mistress, who loves me with all the desperation of passion to which she would fall a sacrifice. But why do I talk as if I were still at liberty to make a choice?—My head is certainly very confused. I forgot that I am bound by a solemn promise, and this is the evil which distracts me. I will give you, if I can, a clear narrative.

Last night I had a terrible scene with Olivia. I foresaw that she would be alarmed by my intended visit to L— Castle, even though it was but to take leave of my Leonora. I abstained from seeing Olivia to avoid altercation, and with all the delicacy in my power I wrote to her, assuring her that my resolution was fixed. Note after note came from her, with pathetic and passionate appeals to my heart; but I was still resolute. At length, the day before that on which I was to set out for L— Castle, she wrote to warn me, that if I wished to take a last farewell, I must see her that evening: her note concluded with, "To-morrow's sun will not rise for Olivia." This threat, and many strange hints of her opinions concerning suicide, I at the time disregarded, as only thrown out to intimidate a lover. However, knowing the violence of Olivia's temper, I was punctual to the appointed hour, fully determined by my firmness to convince her that these female wiles were vain.

My dear friend, I would not advise the wisest man and the most courageous upon earth to risk such dangers, confident in his strength. Even a victory may cost him too dear.

I found Olivia reclining on a sofa, her beautiful tresses unbound, her dress the perfection of elegant negligence. I half suspected that it was studied negligence: yet I could not help pausing, as I entered, to contemplate a figure. She never looked more beautiful—more fascinating. Holding out her hand to me, she said, with her languid smile, and tender expression of voice and manner, "You are come then to bid me farewell. I doubted whether... But I will not upbraid—mine be all the pain of this last adieu. During the few minutes we have to pass together,

"'Between us two let there be peace.'"

I sat down beside her, rather agitated, I confess, but commanding myself so that my emotion could not be visible. In a composed tone I asked, why she spoke of a last adieu? and observed that we should meet again in a few days.

"Never!" replied Olivia. "Weak woman as I am, love inspires me with sufficient force to make and to keep this resolution."

As she spoke, she took from her bosom a rose, and presenting it to me in a solemn manner, "Put this rose into water to-night," continued she; "to-morrow it will be alive!"

Her look, her expressive eyes, seemed to say, this flower will be alive, but Olivia will be dead. I am ashamed to confess that I was silent, because I could not just then speak.

"I have used some precaution," resumed Olivia, "to spare you, my dearest L—, unnecessary pain.—Look around you."

The room, I now for the first time observed, was ornamented with flowers.

"This apartment, I hope," continued she, "has not the air of the chamber of death. I have endeavoured to give it a festive appearance, that the remembrance of your last interview with your once loved Olivia may be at least unmixed with horror."

At this instant, my dear general, a confused recollection of Rousseau's Heloise, the dying scene, and her room ornamented with flowers, came into my imagination, and destroying the idea of reality, changed suddenly the whole course of my feelings.

In a tone of raillery I represented to Olivia her resemblance to Julie, and observed that it was a pity she had not a lover whose temper was more similar than mine to that of the divine St. Preux. Stung to the heart by my ill-timed raillery, Olivia started up from the sofa, broke from my arms with sudden force, snatched from the table a penknife, and plunged it into her side.

She was about to repeat the blow, but I caught her arm—she struggled—"promise me, then," cried she, "that you will never more see my hated rival."

"I cannot make such a promise, Olivia," said I, holding her uplifted arm forcibly. "I will not."

The words "hated rival," which showed me that Olivia was actuated more by the spirit of hatred than love, made me reply in as decided a tone as even you could have spoken, my dear general. But I was shocked, and reproached myself with cruelty, when I saw the blood flow from her side: she was terrified. I took the knife from her powerless hand, and she fainted in my arms. I had sufficient presence of mind to reflect that what had happened should be kept as secret as possible; therefore, without summoning Josephine, whose attachment to her mistress I have reason to suspect, I threw open the windows, gave Olivia air and water, and her senses returned: then I despatched my Swiss for a surgeon. I need not speak of my own feelings—no suspense could be more dreadful than that which I endured between the sending for the surgeon and the moment when he gave his opinion. He relieved me at once, by pronouncing it to be a slight flesh wound, that would be of no manner of consequence. Olivia, however, whether from alarm or pain, or from the sight of the blood, fainted three times during the dressing of her side; and though the surgeon assured her that it would be perfectly well in a few days, she was evidently apprehensive that we concealed from her the real danger. At the idea of the approach of death, which now took possession of her imagination, all courage forsook her, and for some time my efforts to support her spirits were ineffectual. She could not dispense with the services of Josephine; and from the moment this French woman entered the room, there was nothing to be heard but exclamations the most violent and noisy. As to assistance, she could give none. At last her exaggerated demonstrations of horror and grief ended with,—"Dieu merci! an moins nous voilà delivrés de ce voyage affreux. Apparemment qu'il ne sera plus question de ce vilain Petersburg pour madame."

A new train of thoughts was roused by these words in Olivia's mind; and looking at me, she eagerly inquired why the journey to Petersburg was to be given up, if she was in no danger? I assured her that Josephine spoke at random, that my intentions with regard to the embassy to Russia were unaltered.

"Seulement retardé un peu," said Josephine, who was intent only upon her own selfish object.—"Sûrement, madame ne voyagera pas dans cet état!"

Olivia started up, and looking at me with terrific wildness in her eyes, "Swear to me," said she, "swear that you will not deceive me, or I will this instant tear open this wound, and never more suffer it to be closed."

"Deceive you, Olivia!" cried I, "what deceit can you fear from me?—What is it you require of me?"

"I require from you a promise, a solemn promise, that you will go with me to Russia!"

"I solemnly promise that I will," said I: "now be tranquil, Olivia, I beseech you."

The surgeon represented the necessity of keeping herself quiet, and declared that he would not answer for the cure of his patient on any other terms. Satisfied by the solemnity of my promise, Olivia now suffered me to depart. This morning she sends me word that in a few days she shall be ready to leave England. Can you meet me, my dear friend, at L— Castle? I go down there to-day, to bid adieu to Leonora. From thence I shall proceed to Yarmouth, and embark immediately. Olivia will follow me.

Your obliged

F. L—.

LETTER XCIII

LEONORA TO HER MOTHER

L— Castle

Dearest Mother,

My husband is here! at home with me, with your happy Leonora—and his heart is with her. His looks, his voice, his manner tell me so, and by them I never was deceived. No, he is incapable of deceit. Whatever have been his errors, he never stooped to dissimulation. He is again my own, still capable of loving me, still worthy of all my affection. I knew that the delusion could not last long, or rather you told me so, my best friend, and I believed you; you did him justice. He was indeed deceived—who might not have been deceived by Olivia? His passions were under the power of an enchantress; but now he has triumphed over her arts. He sees her such as she is, and her influence ceases.

I am not absolutely certain of all this; but I believe, because I hope it: yet he is evidently embarrassed, and seems unhappy: what can be the meaning of this? Perhaps he does not yet know his Leonora sufficiently to be secure of her forgiveness. How I long to set his heart at ease, and to say to him, let the past be forgotten for ever! How easy it is to the happy to forgive! There have been moments when I could not, I fear, have been just, when I am sure that I could not have been generous. I shall immediately offer to accompany Mr. L— to Russia; I can have no farther hesitation, for I see that he wishes it; indeed, just now he almost said so. His baggage is already embarked at Yarmouth—he sails in a few days—and in a few hours your daughter's fate, your daughter's happiness, will be decided. It is decided, for I am sure he loves me; I see, I hear, I feel it. Dearest mother, I write to you in the first moment of joy.—I hear his foot upon the stairs.

Your happy

LEONORA L—.

LEONORA TO HER MOTHER

L— Castle.

MY DEAR MOTHER,

My hopes are all vain. Your prophecies will never be accomplished. We have both been mistaken in Mr. L—'s character, and henceforward your daughter must not depend upon him for any portion of her happiness. I once thought it impossible that my love for him could be diminished: he has changed my opinion. Mine is not that species of weak or abject affection which can exist under the sense of ill-treatment and injustice, much less can my love survive esteem for its object.

I told you, my dear mother, and I believed, that his affections had returned to me; but I was mistaken. He has not sufficient strength or generosity of soul to love me, or to do justice to my love. I offered to go with him to Russia: he answered, "That is impossible."—Impossible!—Is it then impossible for him to do that which is just or honourable? or seeing what is right, must he follow what is wrong? or can his heart never more be touched by virtuous affections? Is his taste so changed, so depraved, that he can now be pleased and charmed only by what is despicable and profligate in our sex? Then I should rejoice that we are to be separated—separated for ever. May years and years pass away and wear out, if possible, the memory of all he has been to me! I think I could better, much better bear the total loss, the death of him I have loved, than endure to feel that he had survived both my affection and esteem; to see the person the same, but the soul changed; to feel every day, every hour, that I must despise what I have so admired and loved.

Mr. L— is gone from hence. He leaves England the day after to-morrow. Lady Olivia is to follow him. I am glad that public decency is not to be outraged by their embarking together. My dearest mother, be assured that at this moment your daughter's feelings are worthy of you. Indignation and the pride of virtue support her spirit.

LEONORA L—.

GENERAL B— TO LADY LEONORA L—.

Yarmouth.

Had I not the highest confidence in Lady Leonora L—'s fortitude, I should not venture to write to her at this moment, knowing as I do that she is but just recovered from a dangerous illness.

Mr. L— had requested me to meet him at L— Castle previously to his leaving England, but it was out of my power. I met him however on the road to Yarmouth, and as we travelled together I had full opportunity of seeing the state of his mind. Permit me—the urgency of the case requires it—to speak without reserve, with the freedom of an old friend. I imagine that your ladyship parted from Mr. L— with feelings of indignation, at which I cannot be surprised: but if you had seen him as I saw him, indignation would have given way to pity. Loving you, madam, as you deserve to be loved, most ardently, most tenderly; touched to his inmost soul by the proofs of affection he had seen in your letters, in your whole conduct, even to the last moment of parting; my unhappy friend felt himself bound to resist the temptation of staying with you, or of accepting your generous offer to accompany him to Petersburg. He thought himself bound in honour by a promise extorted from him to save from suicide one whom he thinks he has injured, one who has thrown herself upon his protection. Of the conflict in his mind at parting with your ladyship I can judge from what he suffered afterwards. I met Mr. L— with feelings of extreme indignation, but before I had been an hour in his company, I never pitied any man so much in my life, for I never yet saw any one so truly wretched, and so thoroughly convinced that he deserved to be so. You know that he is not one who often gives way to his emotions, not one who expresses them much in words—but he could not command his feelings.

The struggle was too violent. I have no doubt that it was the real cause of his present illness. As the moment approached when he was to leave England, he became more and more agitated. Towards evening he sunk into a sort of apathy and gloomy silence, from which he suddenly broke into delirious raving. At twelve o'clock last night, the night he was to have sailed, he was seized with a violent and infectious fever. As to the degree of immediate danger, the physicians here cannot yet pronounce. I have sent to town for Dr. —. Your ladyship may he certain that I shall not quit my friend, and that he shall have every possible assistance and attendance.

I am, with the truest esteem,

Your ladyship's faithful servant,

J. B.

LEONORA TO HER MOTHER.

DEAR MOTHER, L— Castle.

This moment an express from General B—. Mr. L— is dangerously ill at Yarmouth—a fever, brought on by the agitation of his mind. How unjust I have been! Forget all I said in my last. I write in the utmost haste—just setting out for Yarmouth. I hope to be there to-morrow.

Your affectionate

LEONORA L—.

I open this to enclose the general's letter, which will explain every thing.

GENERAL B— TO THE DUCHESS OF —.

MY DEAR MADAM, Yarmouth.

Your Grace, I find, is apprised of Lady Leonora L—'s journey hither: I fear that you rely upon my prudence for preventing her exposing herself to the danger of catching this dreadful fever. But that has been beyond my power. Her ladyship arrived late last night. I had foreseen the probability of her coming, but not the possibility of her coming so soon. I had taken no precautions, and she was in the house and upon the stairs in an instant. No entreaties, no arguments could stop her; I assured her that Mr. L—'s fever was pronounced by all the physicians to be of the most infectious kind. Dr. — joined me in representing that she would expose her life to almost certain danger if she persisted in her determination to see her husband; but she pressed forward, regardless of all that could be said. To the physicians she made no answer; to me she replied, "You are Mr. L—'s friend, but I am his wife: you have not feared to hazard your life for him, and do you think I can hesitate?" I urged that there was no necessity for more than one person's running this hazard; and that since it had fallen to my lot to be with my friend when he was first taken ill—She interrupted me,—"Is not this taking a cruel advantage of me, general? You know that I, too, would have been with Mr. L—, if—if it had been possible." Her manner, her pathetic emphasis, and the force of her implied meaning, struck me so much, that I was silent, and suffered her to pass on; but again the idea of her danger rushing upon my mind, I sprang before her to the door of Mr. L—'s apartment, and opposed her entrance. "Then, general," said she, calmly, "perhaps you mistake me—perhaps you have heard repeated some unguarded words of mine in the moment of indignation ... unjust ... you best know how unjust indignation!—and you infer from these that my affection for my husband is extinguished. I deserve this—but do not punish me too severely."

I still kept my hand upon the lock of the door, expostulating with Lady Leonora in your Grace's name, and in Mr. L—'s, assuring her that if he were conscious of what was passing, and able to speak, he would order me to prevent her seeing him in his present situation.

"And you, too, general!" said she, bursting into tears: "I thought you were my friend—would you prevent me from seeing him? And is not he conscious of what is passing? And is not he able to speak? Sir, I must be admitted! You have done your duty—now let me do mine. Consider, my right is superior to yours. No power on earth should or can prevent a wife from seeing her husband when he is.... Dear, dear general!" said she, clasping her raised hands, and falling suddenly at my feet, "let me see him but for one minute, and I will be grateful to you for ever!"

I could resist no longer—I tremble for the consequences. I know your Grace sufficiently to be aware that you ought to be told the whole truth. I have but little hopes of my poor friend's life.

With much respect,

Your grace's faithful servant,

J.B.

LETTER XCVIII

OLIVIA TO MR. L—.

Richmond.

A mist hung over my eyes, and "my ears with hollow murmurs rung," when the dreadful tidings of your alarming illness were announced by your cruel messenger. My dearest L—! why does inexorable destiny doom me to be absent from you at such a crisis? Oh! this fatal wound of mine! It would, I fear, certainly open again if I were to travel. So this corporeal being must be imprisoned here, while my anxious soul, my viewless spirit, hovers near you, longing to minister each tender consolation, each nameless comfort that love alone can, with fond prescience and magic speed, summon round the couch of pain.

"O that I had the wings of a dove, that I might fly to you!" Why must I resign the sweetly-painful task of soothing you in the hour of sickness? And shall others with officious zeal,

"Guess the faint wish, explain the asking eye?"

Alas it must be so—even were I to fly to him, my sensibility could not support the scene. To behold him stretched on the bed of disease—perhaps of death—would be agony past endurance. Let firmer nerves than Olivia's, and hearts more callous, assume the offices from which they shrink not. 'Tis the fate, the hard fate of all endued with exquisite sensibility, to be palsied by the excess of their feelings, and to become imbecile at the moment their exertions are most necessary.

Your too tenderly sympathizing

OLIVIA.

LETTER XCIX

LEONORA TO HER MOTHER.

Yarmouth.

My husband is alive, and that is all. Never did I see, nor could I have conceived, such a change, and in so short a time! When I opened the door, his eyes turned upon me with unmeaning eagerness: he did not know me. The good general thought my voice might have some effect. I spoke, but could obtain no answer, no sign of intelligence. In vain I called upon him by every name that used to reach his heart. I kneeled beside him, and took one of his burning hands in mine. I kissed it, and suddenly he started up, exclaiming, "Olivia! Olivia!" with dreadful vehemence. In his delirium he raved about Olivia's stabbing herself, and called upon us to hold her arm, looking wildly towards the foot of the bed, as if the figure were actually before him. Then he sunk back, as if quite exhausted, and gave a deep sigh. Some of my tears fell upon his hand; he felt them before I perceived that they had fallen, and looked so earnestly in my face, that I was in hopes his recollection was returning; but he only said, "Olivia, I believe that you love me;" then sighed more deeply than before, drew his hand away from me, and, as well as I could distinguish, said something about Leonora.

But why should I give you the pain of hearing all these circumstances, my dear mother? It is enough to say, that he passed a dreadful night. This morning the physicians say, that if he passes this night—if—my dear mother, what a terrible suspense!

LEONORA L—.

LETTER C

LEONORA TO HER MOTHER.

Yarmouth.

Morning is at last come, and my husband is still alive: so there is yet hope. When I said I thought I could bear to survive him, how little I knew of myself, and how little, how very little I expected to be so soon tried! All evils are remediable but one, that one which I dare not name.

The physicians assure me that he is better. His friend, to whose judgment I trust more, thinks as they do. I know not what to believe. I dread to flatter myself and to be disappointed, I will write again, dearest mother, to-morrow.

Your ever affectionate

LEONORA L—.

LETTER CI

LEONORA TO HER MOTHER.

Wednesday.

No material change since yesterday, my dear mother. This morning, as I was searching for some medicine, I saw on the chimney-piece a note from Lady Olivia —. It might have been there yesterday, and ever since my arrival, but I did not see it. At any other time it would have excited my indignation, but my mind is now too much weakened by sorrow. My fears for my husband's life absorb all other feelings.

LETTER CII

OLIVIA TO MR. L—.

Richmond.

Words cannot express what I have suffered since I wrote last! Oh! why do I not bear that the danger is over!—Long since would I have been with you, all that my soul holds dear, could I have escaped from these tyrants, these medical despots, who detain me by absolute force, and watch over me with unrelenting vigilance. I have consulted Dr. —, who assures me that my fears of my wound opening, were I to take so long a journey, are too well-founded; that in the present feverish state of my mind he would not answer for the consequences. I heed him not—life I value not.—Most joyfully would I sacrifice myself for the man I love. But even could I escape from my persecutors, too well I know that to see you would be a vain attempt—too well I know that I should not be admitted. Your love, your fears for Olivia would barbarously banish her, and forbid her your dear, your dangerous atmosphere. Too justly would you urge that my rashness might prove our mutual ruin—that in the moment of crisis or of convalescence, anxiety for me might defeat the kind purpose of nature. And even were I secure of your recovery, the delay, I speak not of the danger of my catching the disease, would, circumstanced as we are, be death to our hopes. We should be compelled to part. The winds would waft you from me. The waves would bear you to another region, far—oh! far from your

OLIVIA.

LETTER CIII

GENERAL B— TO THE DUCHESS OF —.

MY DEAR MADAM, Yarmouth, Thursday,—.

Mr. L— has had a relapse, and is now more alarmingly ill than I have yet seen him: he does not know his situation, for his delirium has returned. The physicians give him over. Dr. H— says that we must prepare for the worst.

I have but one word of comfort for your Grace—that your admirable daughter's health has not yet suffered.

Your Grace's faithful servant,

J.B.

LEONORA TO HER MOTHER.

MY DEAREST MOTHER, Yarmouth.

The delirium has subsided. A few minutes ago, as I was kneeling beside him, offering up an almost hopeless prayer for his recovery, his eyes opened, and I perceived that he knew me. He closed his eyes again without speaking, opened them once more, and then looking at me fixedly, exclaimed: "It is not a dream! You are Leonora!—my Leonora!"

What exquisite pleasure I felt at the sound of these words, at the tone in which they were pronounced! My husband folded me in his arms; and, till I felt his burning lips, I forgot that he was ill.

When he came thoroughly to his recollection, and when the idea that his fever might be infectious occurred to him, he endeavoured to prevail upon me to leave the room. But what danger can there be for me now? My whole soul, my whole frame is inspired with new life. If he recover, your daughter may still be happy.

GENERAL B—TO THE DUCHESS OF—.

My Dear Madam,

A few hours ago my friend became perfectly sensible of his danger, and calling me to his bedside, told me that he was eager to make use of the little time which he might have to live. He was quite calm and collected. He employed me to write his last wishes and bequests; and I must do him the justice to declare, that the strongest idea and feeling in his mind evidently was the desire to show his entire confidence in his wife, and to give her, in his last moments, proofs of his esteem and affection. When he had settled his affairs, he begged to be left alone for some time. Between twelve and one his bell rang, and he desired to see Lady Leonora and me. He spoke to me with that warmth of friendship which he has ever felt from our childhood. Then turning to his wife, his voice utterly failed, and he could only press to his lips that hand which was held out to him in speechless agony.

"Excellent woman!" he articulated at last; then collecting his mind, he exclaimed, "My beloved Leonora, I will not die without expressing my feelings for you; I know yours for me. I do not ask for that forgiveness which your generous heart granted long before I deserved it. Your affection for me has been shown by actions, at the hazard of your life; I can only thank you with weak words. You possess my whole heart, my esteem, my admiration, my gratitude."

Lady Leonora, at the word gratitude, made an effort to speak, and laid her hand upon her husband's lips. He added, in a more enthusiastic tone, "You have my undivided love. Believe in the truth of these words—perhaps they are the last I may ever speak."

My friend sunk back exhausted, and I carried Lady Leonora out of the room.

I returned half an hour ago, and found every thing silent: Mr. L— is lying with his eyes closed—quite still—I hope asleep. This may be a favourable crisis. I cannot delay this letter longer.

Your Grace's faithful servant,

J. B.

LETTER CVI

LEONORA TO HER MOTHER.

DEAREST MOTHER, Yarmouth.

He has slept several hours.—Dr. H—, the most skilful of all his physicians, says that we may now expect his recovery. Adieu. The good general will add a line to assure you that I am not deceived, nor too sanguine.

Yours most affectionately,

LEONORA L—.

Postscript by General B—.

I have some hopes—that is all I can venture to say to your grace.

LETTER CVII

LEONORA TO HER MOTHER.

DEAREST MOTHER, Yarmouth.

Excellent news for you to-day!—Mr. L— is pronounced out of danger. He seems excessively touched by my coming here, and so grateful for the little kindness I have been able to show him during his illness!

But alas! that fatal promise! the recollection of it comes across my mind like a spectre. Mr. L— has never touched upon this subject,—I do all in my power to divert his thoughts to indifferent objects.

This morning when I went into his room, I found him tearing to pieces that note which I mentioned to you a few days ago. He seemed much agitated, and desired to see General B—. They are now together, and were talking so loud in the next room to me, that I was obliged to retire, lest I should overhear secrets. Mr. L— this moment sends for me. If I should not have time to add more, this short letter will satisfy you for to-day.

Leonora L—.

I open my letter to say, that I am not so happy as I was when I began it. I have heard all the circumstances relative to this terrible affair. Mr. L— will go to Russia. I am as far from happiness as ever.

OLIVIA TO MR. L—.

Richmond.

"Say, is not absence death to those that love?"

How just, how beautiful a sentiment! yet cold and callous is that heart which knows not that there is a pang more dreadful than absence—far as the death of lingering torture exceeds, in corporeal sufferance, the soft slumber of expiring nature. Suspense! suspense! compared with thy racking agony, even absence is but the blessed euthanasia of love.

My dearest L—, why this torturing silence? one line, one word, I beseech you, from your own hand; say but I live and love you, my Olivia. Hour after hour, and day after day, have I waited and waited, and hoped, and feared to hear from you. Oh, this intolerable agonizing suspense! Yet hope clings to my fond heart—hope! sweet treacherous hope!

"Non so si la Speranza
Va con l'inganno unita;
So che mantiene in vita
Qualche infelici almen."

Olivia.

MR. L— TO OLIVIA.

MY DEAR OLIVIA, Yarmouth.

This is the first line I have written since my illness. I could not sooner relieve you from suspense, for during most of this time I have been delirious, and never till now able to write. My physicians have this morning pronounced me out of danger; and as soon as my strength is sufficient to bear the voyage, I shall sail, according to my promise.

Your prudence, or that of your physician, has saved me much anxiety—perhaps saved my life: for had you been so rash as to come hither, besides my fears for your safety, I should have been exposed, in the moment of my returning reason, to a conflict of passions which I could not have borne.

Leonora is with me; she arrived the night after I was taken ill, and forced her way to me, when my fever was at the highest, and while I was in a state of delirium.

Lady Leonora will stay with me till the moment I sail, which I expect to do in about ten days. I cannot say positively, for I am still very weak, and may not be able to keep my word to a day. Adieu. I hope your mind will now be at ease. I am glad to hear from the surgeon that your wound is quite closed. I will write again, and more fully, when I am better able. Believe me, Olivia, I am most anxious to secure your happiness: allow me to believe that this will be in the power of

Yours sincerely,

F. L—.

LETTER CX

OLIVIA TO MR. L—.

Richmond.

Barbarous man! with what cold cruelty you plunge a dagger into my heart! Leonora is with you!—Leonora! Then I am undone. Yes, she will—she has resumed all her power, her rights, her habitual empire over your heart. Wretched Olivia!—But you say it is your wish to secure my happiness, you bid me allow you to believe it is in your power. What phrases!—You will sail, according to your promise.—Then nothing but your honour binds you to Olivia. And even now, at this guilty instant, in your secret soul, you wish, you expect from my offended pride, from my disgusted delicacy, a renunciation of this promise, a release from all the ties that bind you to me. You are right: this is what I ought to do; what I would do, if love had not so weakened my soul, so prostrated my spirit, rendered me so abject a creature, that I cannot what I would.

I must love on—female pride and resentment call upon me in vain. I cannot hate you. Even by the feeble tie, which I see you long to break, I must hold rather than let you go for ever. I will not renounce your promise. I claim it. I adjure you by all which a man of honour holds most sacred, to quit England the moment your health will allow you to sail. No equivocating with your conscience!—I hold you to your word. Oh, my dearest L—! to feel myself reduced to use such language to you, to find myself clinging to that last resource of ship-wrecked love, a promise! It is with unspeakable agony I feel all this; lower I cannot sink in misery. Raise me, if indeed you wish my happiness—raise me! it is yet in your power. Tell me, that my too susceptible heart has mistaken phantoms for realities—tell me, that your last was not colder than usual; yes, I am ready to be deceived. Tell me that it was only the languor of disease; assure me that my rival forced her way only to your presence, that she has not won her easy way back to your heart—assure me that you are impatient once more to see your own

OLIVIA.

LETTER CXI

LEONORA TO HER MOTHER.

MY DEAREST MOTHER, Yarmouth.

Can you believe or imagine that I am actually unwilling to say or to think that Mr. L— is quite well? yet this is the fact. Such is the inconsistency and weakness of our natures—of my nature, I should say. But a short time ago I thought that no evil could be so great as his danger; now that danger is past, I dread to hear him say that he is perfectly recovered. The moment he is able he goes to Russia; that is decided irrevocably. The promise has been claimed and repeated. A solemn promise cannot be broken for any human consideration. I should despise him if he broke it; but can I love him for keeping it? His mind is at this instant agitated as much as mine is—more it cannot be. Yet I ought to be better able to part with him now than when we parted before, because I have now at least the consolation of knowing that he leaves me against his will—that his heart will not go from me. This time I cannot be deceived; I have had the most explicit assurances of his undivided love. And indeed I was never deceived. All the appearances of regret at parting with me were genuine. The general witnessed the consequent struggle in Mr. L—'s mind, and this fever followed.

I will endeavour to calm and content myself with the possession of his love, and with the assurance that he will return to me as soon as possible. As soon as possible! but what a vague hope! He sails with the first fair wind. What a dreadful certainty! Perhaps to-morrow! Oh, my dearest mother, perhaps to-night!

LEONORA L—.

LETTER CXII

GENERAL B— TO THE DUCHESS OF —.

MY DEAR MADAM, Yarmouth.

Today Mr. L—, finding himself sufficiently recovered, gave orders to all his suite to embark, and the wind being fair, determined to go on board immediately. In the midst of the bustle of the preparations for his departure, Lady Leonora, exhausted by her former activity, and unable to take any part in what was passing, sat silent, pale, and motionless, opposite to a window, which looked out upon the sea; the vessel in which her husband was to sail lay in sight, and her eyes were fixed upon the streamers, watching their motion in the wind.

Mr. L— was in his own apartment writing letters. An express arrived; and among other letters for the English ambassador to Russia, there was a large packet directed to Lady Leonora L—. Upon opening it, the crimson colour flew into her face, and she exclaimed, "Olivia's letters!—Lady Olivia —'s letters to Mad. de P—. Who could send these to me?"

"I give you joy with all my heart!" cried I; "no matter how they come—they come in the most fortunate moment possible. I would stake my life upon it they will unmask Olivia at once. Where is Mr. L—? He must read them this moment."

I was hurrying out of the room to call my friend, but Lady Leonora stopped my career, and checked the transport of my joy.

"You do not think, my dear general," said she, "that I would for any consideration do so dishonourable an action as to read these letters?"

"Only let Mr. L— read them," interrupted I, "that is all I ask of your ladyship. Give them to me. For the soul of me I can see nothing dishonourable in this. Let Lady Olivia be judged by her own words. Your ladyship shall not be troubled with her trash, but give the letters to me, I beseech you."

"No, I cannot," said Lady Leonora, steadily. "It is a great temptation; but I ought not to yield." She deliberately folded them up in a blank cover, directed them to Lady Olivia, and sealed them; whilst I, half in admiration and half in anger, went on expostulating.

"Good God! this is being too generous! But, my dear Lady Leonora, why will you sacrifice yourself? This is misplaced delicacy! Show those letters, and I'll lay my life Mr. L— never goes to Russia."

"My dear friend," said she, looking up with tears in her eyes, "do not tempt me beyond my power to resist. Say no more." At this instant Mr. L— came into the room; and I am ashamed to confess to your Grace, I really was so little master of myself, that I was upon the point of seizing Olivia's letters, and putting them into his hands. "L—," said I, "here is your admirable wife absurdly, yes, I must say it, absurdly standing upon a point of honour with one who has none! That packet which she has before her—"

Lady Leonora imposed silence upon me by one of those looks which no man can resist.

"My dear Leonora, you are right," said Mr. L—; "and you are almost right, my dear general: I know what that packet contains; and without doing anything dishonourable, I hold myself absolved from my promise; I shall not go to Russia, my dearest wife!" He flew into her arms—and I left them. I question whether they either of them felt much more than I did.

For some minutes I was content with knowing that these things had really happened, that I had heard Mr. L— say he was absolved from all promises, and that he would not go to Russia; but how did all this happen so suddenly?—How did he know the contents of Olivia's letters, and without doing any thing dishonourable? There are some people who cannot be perfectly happy till they know the rationale of their happiness. I am one of these. I did not feel "a sober certainty of waking bliss," till I read a letter which Mr. L— received by the same express that brought Olivia's letters, and which he read while we were debating. I beg your Grace's pardon if I am too minute in explanation; but I do as I would be done by. The letter was from one of the private secretaries, who is, I understand, a relation and friend of Lady Leonora L—. As the original goes this night to Lady Olivia, I send your Grace a copy. You will give me credit for copying, and at such a time as this! I congratulate your Grace, and

I have the honour to be, &c.,

J. B.

LETTER CXIII

TO MR. L—

[Private.]

London, St. James's-street.

My Dear Sir,

In the same moment you receive this, your lady, for whom I have the highest regard, will receive from me a valuable present, a packet of Lady Olivia —'s letters to one of her French friends. These letters were lately found in a French frigate, taken by one of our cruisers; and, as intercepted correspondence is the order of the day, these, with all the despatches on board, were transmitted to our office to be examined, in hopes of making reprisals of state secrets. Some letters about the court and Emperor of Russia led us to suppose that we should find some political manoeuvres, and we examined farther. The examination fortunately fell to my lot, as private secretary. After looking them all over, however, I found that these papers contain only family secrets: I obtained permission to send them to Lady Leonora L—, to ensure the triumph of virtue over vice—to put it into her ladyship's power completely to unmask her unworthy rival. These letters will show you by what arts you have been deceived. You will find yourself ridiculed as a cold, awkward Englishman; one who will hottentot again, whatever pains may be taken to civilize him; a man of ice, to be taken as a lover from pure charity, or pure curiosity, or the pure besoin d'aimer. Here are many pure motives, of which you will, my dear sir, take your choice. You will farther observe in one of her letters, that Lady Olivia premeditated the design of prevailing with you to carry her to Russia, that she might show her power to that proudest of earthly prudes, the Duchess of —, and that she might gratify her great revenge against Lady Leonora L—.

Sincerely hoping, my dear sir, that these letters may open your eyes, and restore you and my amiable relation to domestic happiness, I make no apology for the liberty I take, and cannot regret the momentary pain I may inflict. You are at liberty to make what use you think proper of this letter.

I have it in command from my Lord — to add, that if your health, or any other circumstances, should render this embassy to Russia less desirable to you than it appeared some time ago, other arrangements can be made, and another friend of government is ready to supply your place.

I am, my dear sir,

Yours, &c.

To F. L—, Esq. &c.

FROM LADY LEONORA — TO THE DUCHESS OF —.

Yarmouth.

Joy, dearest mother! Come and share your daughter's happiness!

Continued by General B—.

Lady Olivia, thus unmasked by her own hand, has fled to the continent, declaring that she will never more return to England. There she is right—England is not a country fit for such women.—But I will never waste another word or thought upon her.

Mr. L— has given up the Russian embassy, and returns with Lady Leonora to L— Castle to-morrow. He has invited me to accompany them. Lady Leonora is now the happiest of wives, and your Grace the happiest of mothers.

I have the honour and the pleasure to be

Your Grace's sincerely attached,

J. B—.

THE DUCHESS OF — TO LADY LEONORA L—.

My beloved daughter, pride and delight of your happy mother's heart, I give you joy! Your temper, fortitude, and persevering affection, have now their just reward. Enjoy your happiness, heightened as it must be by the sense of self-approbation, and by the sympathy of all who know you. And now let me indulge the vanity of a mother; let me exult in the accomplishment of my prophecies, and let me be listened to with due humility, when I prophesy again. With as much certainty as I foretold what is now present, I foresee, my child, your future destiny, and I predict that you will preserve while you live your husband's fondest affections. Your prudence will prevent you from indulging too far your taste for retirement, or for the exclusive society of your intimate friends. Spend your winters in London: your rank, your fortune, and, I may be permitted to add, your character, manners, and abilities, give you the power of drawing round you persons of the best information and of the highest talents. Your husband will find, in such society, every thing that can attach him to his home; and in you, his most rational friend and his most charming companion, who will excite him to every generous and noble exertion.

For the good and wise, there is in love, a power unknown to the ignorant and the vicious, a power of communicating fresh energy to all the faculties of the soul, of exalting them to the highest state of perfection. The friendship which in later life succeeds to such love is perhaps the greatest, and certainly the most permanent blessing of life.

An admirable German writer—you see, my dear, that I have no prejudices against good German writers—an admirable German writer says, that "Love is like the morning shadows, which diminish as the day advances; but friendship is like the shadows of the evening, which increase even till the setting of the sun."

—

Maria Edgeworth – A Short Biography

Maria Edgeworth was born at Black Bourton, Oxfordshire on January 1st 1768, the second child of Richard Lovell Edgeworth and Anna Maria Edgeworth (née Elers).

Her early years were with her mother's family in England. Sadly, her mother died when Maria was only five. When her father married his second wife, Honora Sneyd, in 1773, the family went to live at his estate, Edgeworthstown, in County Longford, Ireland.

Maria was later sent to Mrs. Lattafière's school in Derby after Honora fell ill in 1775. There she studied dancing, French and other subjects. After Honora died in 1780 Maria's father married Honora's sister, Elizabeth, causing much social disapproved.

Maria transferred to Mrs. Devis's school in Upper Wimpole Street, London. Her father began to focus more attention on Maria in 1781 when she nearly lost her sight to an eye infection.

She returned home to Ireland at 14, and took charge of her younger siblings. She herself was home-tutored by her father in Irish economics and politics, science, literature and law. Despite her youth literature was in her blood.

She became her father's assistant in managing the Edgeworthstown estate, which had become run-down during the family's absence. Maria would now live and write there for the rest of her life.

With her father she began a lifelong academic collaboration. She meticulously detailed daily Irish life; a valuable lodestone of references for later use in her novels. Maria mixed with the Anglo-Irish gentry, and her aunt, Margaret Ruxton of Blackcastle, supplied her with the novels of Anne Radcliffe and William Godwin and encouraged her ambition to write.

Edgeworth's first published work in 1795 was 'Letters for Literary Ladies'. That same year 'An Essay on the Noble Science of Self-Justification', written for a female audience, states that the fair sex is endowed with an art of self-justification and women should use their gifts to continually challenge the force and power of men, especially their husbands, with wit and intelligence.

In 1796 her first children's book, 'The Parent's Assistant', which included the much loved short story 'The Purple Jar' was published.

In 1798 her father married for the fourth and last time, this time to Frances Beaufort. Frances was a year younger than Maria and they quickly became close.

'Practical Education' (1798) is a progressive work on education that combines the ideas of Locke and Rousseau with scientific inquiry. Edgeworth believed that "learning should be a positive experience and that the discipline of education is more important during the formative years than the acquisition of knowledge." The ultimate goal of Edgeworth's system was to create an independent thinker who understands the consequences of his or her actions.

Her first novel, 'Castle Rackrent' (1800) was published anonymously without her father's knowledge. It was an immediate success and firmly established Maria's appeal to the public.

'Belinda' (1801), was her first full-length novel. It dealt with love, courtship, and marriage, and she examined these as conflicts within her "own personality and environment; conflicts between reason and feeling, restraint and individual freedom, and society and free spirit." Startlingly, 'Belinda' also included a depiction of interracial marriage between an African servant and an English farm-girl. Later editions of the novel, in line with unforgiving times, removed these sections.

Frances also pushed the family to travel more first London (1800), the Midlands (1802) and later the continent; first to Brussels and then to France. They met all the notables, with Maria even receiving a proposal of marriage from a Swedish courtier.

'Tales of Fashionable Life' (1809 and 1812) is a 2-series collection of short stories that often had its focus on the life of women. The second series was so successful that she was now the most commercially successful novelist of her age and ranked alongside her contemporaries Jane Austen and Sir Walter Scott.

On a visit to London in 1813, she met many notables including Lord Byron. She entered into a long correspondence with Sir Walter Scott after the publication of 'Waverley' in 1814, in which he acknowledged her influence, and they formed a lasting friendship. She visited him in Scotland at Abbotsford House in 1823 and the following year he visited Edgeworthstown.

After debating the issue with the economist David Ricardo, Maria came to believe that better management and the further use of science in agriculture would raise food production and help to lower prices. They were both in favour of Catholic Emancipation, enfranchisement for Catholics without property restrictions, agricultural reform and increased educational opportunities for women.

She worked particularly hard to improve the living standards of the poor in Edgeworthstown and to provide schools for the local children whatever their denomination.

After her father's death in 1817 she edited his memoirs, and extended them with her biographical addenda. Her father had married 4 times and sired 22 children. At the height of her creative endeavours, Maria had written, "Seriously it was to please my Father I first exerted myself to write, to please him I continued."

Maria worked for the relief of the famine-stricken Irish peasants during the Irish Potato Famine. She wrote 'Orlandino' and gave the proceeds to the Relieve Fund. However, during the famine her 'business head' insisted that only those tenants who had paid their full rent would receive any relief. She also punished any tenants who voted against her Tory preferences.

'Helen' (1834) is Maria Edgeworth's final novel, the only one she wrote after her father's death. Here the focus was on characters and situation and not moral lessons.

William Rowan Hamilton was elected president of the Royal Irish Academy and Maria's advice was constantly sought especially regarding literature in Ireland. She suggested that women should be allowed to participate in Academy events. Hamilton made Maria an honorary member in 1837.

After a visit to see her relations Maria was struck with severe chest pains and died suddenly of a heart attack in Edgeworthstown on 22nd May 1849. She was 81.

Maria Edgeworth is buried in the family tomb at St. John's Church, Edgeworthstown, Longford, Ireland.

Maria Edgeworth – A Concise Bibliography

Letters for Literary Ladies (1795) Second Edition (1798)
An Essay on the Noble Science of Self-Justification (1795)
The Parent's Assistant (1796)
Practical Education (1798) (2 Vols; collaborated with her father and step-mother)
Castle Rackrent (1800) Novel
Early Lessons (1801)
Moral Tales (1801)
Belinda (1801) Novel
The Mental Thermometer (1801)
Essay on Irish Bulls (1802)
Popular Tales (1804)
The Modern Griselda (1804)
Moral Tales for Young People (1805) (6 Vols)
Leonora (1806)
Essays in Professional Education (1809)
Tales of Fashionable Life (1809)
Ennui (1809) Novel
The Absentee (1812) Novel
Patronage (1814) Novel
Harrington (1817) Novel
Ormond (1817) Novel
Comic Dramas (1817)
Memoirs of Richard Lovell Edgeworth (1820) Editor
Rosamond: A Sequel to Early Lessons (1821)

Frank: A Sequel to Frank in Early Lessons (1822)
Tomorrow (1823) Novel
Helen (1834) novel
Orlandino (1848) Temperance novel